Again, the Dawn

BOOKS BY GRACE SCHULMAN

POETRY

Again, the Dawn: New and Selected Poems, 1976–2022
The Marble Bed
Without a Claim
The Broken String
Days of Wonder: New and Selected Poems
The Paintings of Our Lives
For That Day Only
Hemispheres
Burn Down the Icons

MEMOIR

Strange Paradise: Portrait of a Marriage

TRANSLATION

Songs of Cifar: Poems (with Ann McCarthy de Zavala) by Pablo Antonio Cuadra
At the Stone of Losses: Poems by T. Carmi

CRITICISM AND ESSAYS

Marianne Moore: The Poetry of Engagement
First Loves and Other Adventures: Essays

EDITIONS

The Poems of Marianne Moore (Authorized Edition)
Mourning Songs: Poems of Sorrow and Beauty
Ezra Pound: A Collection of Criticism

Grace Schulman

Again, the Dawn
NEW AND SELECTED POEMS, 1976–2022

TURTLE POINT PRESS
BROOKLYN, NEW YORK

Copyright © 2022 by Grace Schulman

All rights reserved. No part of this book may be reproduced or transmitted in any form by any means, electronic or mechanical, including photocopying, recording, or any information storage and retrieval system, except as may be expressly permitted in writing from the publisher.

Requests for permission to make copies of any part of the work should be sent to:
Turtle Point Press, 208 Java Street, Fifth Floor, Brooklyn, NY 11222
info@turtlepointpress.com

Library of Congress Control Number: 2022941671

Design by Phil Kovacevich

ISBN: 978-1-885983-33-6

Printed in the United States of America

First Edition

For Richard Howard

For every poet it is always morning in the world.

— DEREK WALCOTT

Not knowing when the Dawn will come,
I open every Door,

— EMILY DICKINSON

CONTENTS

New Poems

3	Invitation
4	Confessions of a Nun
6	Letter from Paul Celan
7	Scallop Shell
9	Tesserae
10	Logs
11	The Monument
12	Lot's Wife
14	Hudson River Music
16	Night Visitor
17	Movie Theater
18	Life Raft
20	Broken Ducks
21	How Little We Know
22	Desperate Measures

FROM *The Marble Bed* (2020)

27	Orchid
29	Happiness
31	The Sand Dancers
32	Fragments of a Marriage
33	The Rooted Bed
34	Meteor

35	Gone
37	Because
38	Image Worship
39	Eve Speaks
40	Francesca Redux
41	After All
42	Light in Genoa
44	Moment in Rapallo
46	Alive and Well: Tomb Sculptures in the Staglieno Cemetery
50	Ascension
52	Agony in the Garden
54	That Summer
55	The Vow
56	Cinderella
57	Dr. John
59	The Rainbow Sign
60	Caregiver
61	Survival in the Woods
63	*From* The Letting Go

from *Without a Claim* (2013)

69	Celebration
70	The Sound
71	Without a Claim
73	Moon Shell
74	Antiques Fair

75	Hurricane
76	Letter Never Sent
79	Street Music, Astor Place
80	Woman on the Ceiling
82	My Father's Watches
84	Havdalah
86	Charles Street Psalm
88	Walking to Elijah
90	Hickories
91	Shadow
92	Yellow
94	At the Physical Therapist's
95	In Praise of Shards
97	Chauvet
98	Love in the Afternoon
100	Whelk
102	Green River
103	Cool Jazz
104	Tattoo

FROM *The Broken String* (2007)

107	The Broken String
109	The Letter B
111	The Fifth of July
112	Query
113	Headstones
115	Blue in Green

116	The Footbridge
117	Kol Nidrei, September 2001
119	First Nights
120	Thelonious Himself
121	Art Tatum at the Gee-Haw Stables
122	The Horror
124	Death
127	From the New World
129	Apples
131	The Row
133	Late Snow
134	In Place of Belief
138	Readers
140	Chosen
141	Walk!
142	Harp Song
143	Waves

FROM *Days of Wonder* (2003)

147	Repentance of an Art Critic, 1925
149	Flags
150	The Last Meeting
151	Jewish Cemetery, Eleventh Street
152	Job's Question on Nevis
153	Grandmother's Sea
154	Steps

FROM *The Paintings of Our Lives* (2001)

- 157 Prayer
- 159 God Speaks
- 160 Eve's Unnaming
- 161 Chaim Soutine
- 162 Poem Ending with a Phrase from the Psalms
- 163 Psalm for an Anniversary
- 164 No Strings
- 165 Blue Dawn
- 166 American Solitude
- 168 *Young Woman Drawing*, 1801
- 169 Margaret Fuller
- 171 The Dancers
- 172 Brooklyn Bridge
- 174 Elegy Written in the Conservatory Garden
- 176 Henry James Revisiting, 1904
- 177 The Designer's Notebook
- 179 The Paintings of Our Lives
- 181 Last Requests

FROM *For That Day Only* (1994)

- 185 For That Day Only
- 188 The Movie
- 190 The Present Perfect
- 192 Footsteps on Lower Broadway
- 195 New Netherland, 1654

197	The Button Box
198	Site:
199	Crossing the Square
200	Notes from Underground: W. H. Auden on the No. 6 Train
201	God's Letters
203	Stone Demons
204	False Move
205	The Wedding
207	Julian of Norwich
208	Rescue in Pescallo
214	El Greco's *Saint James, the Less*
215	Carrion
217	The Good Women

FROM *Hemispheres* (1984)

221	Blessed Is the Light
222	Let There Be Translators!
223	Sutton Hoo Ship Burial
225	Morning Song
226	The Stars and the Moon
227	The Flight

FROM *Burn Down the Icons* (1976)

231   The Abbess of Whitby
232   Written on a Road Map
233   Names
234   Street Dance in Barcelona
235   Surely as Certainty Changes
236   Poetry Editor
238   The Examination: Remembrance of Words Lost
241   In the Country of Urgency, There Is a Language
243   Burn Down the Icons
245   Letter to Helen

249   *Notes*
255   *Acknowledgments*

Again, the Dawn

New Poems

Invitation

Dive under a wave,
sink past kelp and wrack
to find plum glass, a teardrop
of a crystal chandelier,

a twist of braided rope
from a sunken ship,
the gold locket you lost,
a healing amethyst,

a stringless dulcimer.
And if you surface now,
come with me while I drift
then rise to read the waves,

note their force and speed,
and ride the breakers in.

Confessions of a Nun

*The speaker is Sister Jacques-Marie,
née Monique Bourgeois.*

Yes, I loved Matisse. He made it for me,
you know, this church of glass and fire.
Now when the sun rolls rectangles on floors

through windows painted yellow, I remember
the yellow broom we stumbled through each morning
when we climbed this hill, and how he stirred

to greens in scrub weeds, whites in the anemones,
and blues in the sliver of sea beyond rock terraces.
He owned his loves. His Vence. I, his Monique.

Nurse. Disciple. Rose. But who was I?
Harsh words we had, a few. I had to leave
for me, myself, my holy vows.

If I belonged to anything, it was
(how could I tell him?), someone larger.
Il faut y avoir plus, there must be more.

Later, he aged, arthritic, waiting for
the angel to wound him. None appeared,
but when my sisters called for a new chapel,

I drew a priest he painted on a wall
while belted to his chair. I tied a brush
to a long twig, strapped it to his arm,

and watched him paint anger in daring strokes:
an outsized poppy, the Virgin and child,
a monk. Rage for lost years, for few to come.

(Why does he think his work is never finished?)
And yet he scorned—what is it?—*pitié*.
Not for him. He told me once, in wartime,

his daughter captured, tortured for her fight
in the *Maquis*, he wept at home, alone—
all the while painting joy in reds and violets.

Now in this blue-green-yellow chapel,
seeing the late day sunlight on the sketches
of planetree, priestly vestments, and an altar

the color of risen bread, I know at last
that just as he held my vows in his great hands,
he, godless, will work it out with God.

Letter from Paul Celan

All gladness, dear Nelly, all light!

Paris to Stockholm: *My dear Nelly.*
After that which happened, the no longer,
your father's hand gripped through barbed wire

then let slip away, your lines still glow
cool as white roses in rain. Fellow survivor,
brother, remember the sudden flash

when we two first met, dazzling the lake?
You, a disbeliever, looked for cause;
I knew it was divine, and prayed

for that gold to come back, as a sign
that we may breathe again in smokeless air.
The fires you saw burn on, even in freedom;

not to have been there magnifies the flame.
For you, though, all that remains of horror
is language washed of horror. In your lines,

white stones, frost, doves, icelight, snowlight,
the lightbringers, star that listens to light.
And in your letter, the lesson is indelible,

after great loss, language is survival—
the fizz of dark waves that crash white
against dull rocks, the secret source of light,

the sun through fog, our not unjoyful days.

Scallop Shell

See them at low tide,
scallop shells glittering on
a scallop-edged shore,

whittled by water
into curvy rows the shape
of waves that kiss the sand

only to erode it. Today
I walked that shoreline, humming,

Camino Santiago,
the road to St. James's tomb,
where pilgrims traveled,

scallop badges on their capes,
and chanted prayers
for a miracle to cure

disease. And so I,
stirred by their purpose,

hunted for scallop shells
shaped like pleated fans,
with mouths that open and close

to steer them from predators.
I scooped up a fan
and blew off sand grains, thinking,

for that one moment,
of how Saint James' body

rose from sea decked with scallops,
and of this empty beach
in another austere time.

Let this unholy pilgrim
implore the scallop shell,

silvery half-moon, save us.

Tesserae

Beach stones tick wet sand like gleaming commas:
ivory eggs, ant-sized silvery beads,
and red-ochre clocks wash in from mountains,

their ancestors. They are — well, forgive me,
chips off the old rocks. Stones are tooled
by the ocean, the master jeweler,

caring the same for quartz and bottle-caps.
Stuck on land, stones cast tear-shaped shadows
that vanish after dark just as my footsteps

disappear with each new wave on shore.
Stone-faced, they conceal an inner wildness
with memories of shipwrecks, cholera,

gulls' broken wings, and shorelines that erode.
In fallow times, I'll scan the sea for answers.
Silence. Then the message of the stones:

outer blankness, inner fire.
The Roman artist who searched for tesserae —
wooden bits, glass shards and cracked shells —

must have known that beach stones, seemingly dull,
would shimmer when grouted in cement
for mosaics, flaming in yellow-gold.

Logs

Giants lie entangled on wet sand,
storm-fallen and hauled out of the sea,
oaks, skin-smooth, naked and unashamed,
crossing each other, touching at the thigh,

one foot wedged between the other's knees,
hidden lovers condemned to cling
in hell, snatched from flight and stuck on shore.
Trees uncrowned, shorn of leaves and branches,

won't wear black veils to mourn great loss;
instead, they boast of shaking out their hair
in dress-up greens, the sap still coursing

through shaded arms, and they remember
leaves kissing across a road. So they live
in raw truth, rot-hollow. Without regret.

The Monument

You walk by ferns, green even in winter,
past workers opening take-out lunches,
to find David Glasgow Farragut,
and ask who was this chesty admiral

who merits a bronze statue with alluring
mermaids, sirens really, carved beneath it,
his jaw set as though he'd walk on water.
Damn the torpedoes, full speed ahead!

Futile now. But look in his eyes and see
a Southerner who fought for the Union's
end to slavery. The guidebooks snub him,
but not my students: in the park one day,

asked to write of anything, they chose him.
Was it the sea, or else the bare-armed beauties;
or did they see a man in a broken country
who sacked his politics for what was right?

Lot's Wife

*Walk. Follow the phosphorescent line
marking the road's edge, even on dark nights,
and watch it glow until you smell the sea.*

After the fires, after the night's alarms,
smoke lingers like a ghost's damp breath.
Don't look back. No. In my mind's eye

are color photos curling black in flames:
my love on bluestone streets trailing shadow,
the charred couch imprinted with his form,

my burned guitar, the strings oddly intact,
the shattered window he began to mend,
the broken wine decanter tipped to pour—

the empty playground swings, U-shaped, like smiles,
car exhaust merged with a breath of lilacs,
the planned walk on a bridge floating in air,

all that we ever had, or might have had.
How the past slinks back unwilled and shining.
Safe now, but safety paid for, at the price

of losing all. As this air clears,
and I see roses flaunt their fuchsia,
where shrieks are gulls, not sirens,

I miss the fumes. Searchlights. Angry winds,
as the moon eclipsed is still the moon,
dark in a sharp circle. Still I'm told,

*God's time runs forward. Observe the ocean
that draws back only to move ahead.*
But when old scraps of talk fly out like cinders,

what is there but regret for words unspoken,
the luminous unknowable, the missed . . .
Damn those warnings. Every survivor

is a witness. I'll turn to the place that was
as I press forward,
                      looking back.

Hudson River Music

In eerie light, I walked between two rivers
that frame my island like a rusty parenthesis,
the East, really an inlet, to the Hudson,

rage-red at sunrise, the path still bare.
Lingering by an ailanthus tree,
I saw a silhouette cut through the mist:

a man sat cross-legged playing a flute,
breathing phrases into the river's silence.
That's when it happened. Now it might have been

the light at dawn, buildings across the drive,
tawny-red brick, ghostlike in mist,
or thinking of Procopius, the Byzantine,

who said an ancient plague had spared no island,
cave, mountain, or wherever they drew breath—
but suddenly the dock was Mesopotamia,

whose name, a rainbow of open vowels,
means "land between two rivers," like my land
running between East River and the Hudson.

A passing tugboat became a barge
for the shah the Sheroe plague was named for.
Then, where the flutist sat, wearing torn jeans,

I saw a robed musician tune a lyre
and sing in emerald tones, *Mysterious protector,*
hold back the plague, compose these waters.

The people raised their hands in supplication.
The tree shimmered at noon. A foghorn bleated.
The river was the Hudson. Nothing changes.

When the gods are cold, raise helpless hands
      and sing out loud.

Night Visitor

I've had more soothing callers at my window.
There's the muse that brushes by as lightly
as a dangling scarf. And airier,
the helium balloon for my neighbor's nuptials,

tied to her guardrail, wafting my way.
Not him. The window demon comes at night
and jabs at a guitar: the jangling discords
and moonless tones call up ferocious joy.

Fingers move crablike on a fretted neck.
He strums the undersides of leaves, roses
the color of blood, silence in the sea's roar.
Hearing those wails, ears that had been dulled

quicken to danger. The quieter muse
blows elegies on a muted trumpet.
Swift angels bless the dead and fly away.
But he lands often, toe-heel, and I tremble.

I tremble all the more when he isn't there.

Movie Theater

No ushers, no grand lobby. Walk downstairs
to many doors, pick one, and hope it's yours,
find a seat and wait for life to change.
Now slide into a soft-shoe with a dancer

dazzled by lights, floating above the floor.
Sweep down a stairwell with the sovereign,
surface from the dream, and be aware
her diamonds are cut glass, her features

make-upped to seem kinder, her lover
an actor who had served a prison term.
On-screen, her heartache was your heartache,
her sins your sins, absolved. The end. Lights on.

The rifle company is downgraded
to soldierly rows of seats. Off-screen,
the moon is dimmer than the studio's kliegs
that silvered castle walls. Observe

how dark the streets are when you lumber home.

Life Raft

Cocktails at 6: a moonbeam chandelier
glittered but cast no light beyond itself,
mirrors hung bare of images. Windows darkened,

merlot sailed on trays. People asked questions
without waiting for answers, without a glance
at one another, as though peering

could tempt the evil eye. But she came closer,
her eyes, black asterisks, demanding more.
Nor could she recall, at first – but then,

What are we doing in these shallows . . . ?
Her voice failed. I wondered why she said it,
neither friend nor stranger. Then I remembered,

years back, at sea one day when rain clouds
crept over dunes, we'd clung to a rubbery life raft—
and talked of what lay hidden below the surf,

her coal eyes zimmering, as though to see
past emerald weeds, and said that after
she'd buckled with the weight of a great loss,

*I found the bottom, sank into it, easy—
but then I hurried back into the light.*
The harsh, abrasive light, she might have added.

And as she spoke, boats faded in mist.
Something spiraled upwards, foam then steam
from fathoms down, a sea creature, perhaps

a stinger. We waited for that mouth
to breathe again, and swam ashore only
after lightning flashed. Back on that shore,

I wished to haul the life raft into a room
of unrevealing stares, and inform the talkers
how one starfish on the sea's dark floor
                    grips luminous rock.

Broken Ducks

Amazing how these ducks with missing parts,
full bodies unseen, recall the wholeness
of painted wooden birds, art of an earlier

America, *one nation indivisible*.
A disembodied beak still shimmers green,
lying on one side like a bright comma

enticing me to half-imagine
the whittled cedar mallard it belonged to;
then there's a decapitated head,

one eye staring above a slender neck.
The fragments were found scattered in a house
once owned by the fisherman whose ancestors,

settlers in this region, chiseled them
to ducklike forms from logs, some say as tokens
of new-world bounty. Ages pass, and now

in your studio, you catch their ruins
penciled in abstract forms: an oblong,
black on white, firmly drawn, promises closure

yet opens on a nubby charcoal shadow.
Speak sketches, say my life is an array
of broken hours, times to be continued . . .

How Little We Know

My friend and I, walking on shore at sundown,
straddle a log and finish our Chablis.
He's shared this wine before with a new love,

fresh as a dune rose, and as explosive
as a breaking wave. Long-married to another,
he wants to leave and stay at the same time.

Love has changed him. Eyes wake to light
as late sun blinks on empty wineglasses
he tucks into a bag that sinks in sand,

weighing him down, like days with no decision.
And that is all. Perhaps the images—
the rose, sunlight on glass, ash from a fire

someone set with twigs the night before—
will stir an ending: loss of a new love
or its green beginning, as you will.

Otherwise, this poem has no solution
and no moral. Not even a judgment,
and I wish it had. Judgment is order.

I have no answer. All I've ever known
is that I'm baffled by life's mystery,
by sudden truth, which makes no sense at all.

Desperate Measures

PHEMIUS

In Ithaca, I improvised cadenzas
at sword-point. My lady's suitors mobbed the palace
and yelled for music. Play, Phemius,

or we'll have your harp. And you. Of course,
she was blameless. The king was gone,
sailing home, we thought, but not entirely

unloved, or not unmoved, along the way.
Her callers waited: harp-song might seduce her.
I gave them halted runs and blurred glissandi.

No flourishes. My lord once blessed my hands
that sent down rain to wash the terrace stones.
For him I'll play. For them I pluck the strings.

DEOR

Good gigs are scarce	and mine were gold.
A fit reward.	When I raised the harp,
strings shimmered,	scops fell silent.
That was then.	Today at court
another singer	seized my chair;
the king who smiled	at his sugary lines
glared at my tales,	gloomy though true.
I frowned like Joseph	fired by Pharoah,
before I shrugged:	*this, too, shall pass.*
You hailed my hour,	my hoard of words;
his name, his dross	will dissolve in air.

IN MESOPOTAMIA

I strum a shining bull, gold paint on wood,
lapis lazuli for beard, seashells for eyes.

In a white robe I play for priestly men
with arms upraised in wonder, and I sing

to lift the plague and heal the king.
Raising the lyre, I'm animal, human, god.

I swell with the bull's divine fertility
until the song ends. Then I'm small again,

a man, low rank. I dream of what I was.

PRISONER

There are no melodies for parents lost,
forced labor camps, boots at the door.
In prison, I dream sounds: cathedral bells,

a carillon, sleigh bells. My mother's harp.
Her green dress as she played, a color bright
as freedom. Sounds rise up and fall like snow

rinsed of impurities. Hear me now.
Listen for what is left out.
Listen for the silences.

FROM *The Marble Bed* (2020)

Orchid

Not raised but found, this dancer, idling on trash,
abandoned in the compactor room,
fated to be smothered in a green bag,

its seven blooms startling, hot pink smiles
in deadpan weather, on the year's shortest
day, with the long night ahead. Gingerly,

sponging off ashes, eggshells, silvery
powder (talc, I hope), from its mossy planter,
I slide it toward high windows, and it changes

like fire: sherry to red-purple to magenta,
colors of blood, of beaujolais, of sin
and holiness, of saints on stained-glass panels,

light shining through, a diva's fan.
Fuchsia, the color named for a plant
that must have jolted Leonhart Fuchs,

the botanist, when he discovered it
in the 16th century, my orchid's
serious name is phalaenopsis,

for moths in flight. Its wingy blooms
blink, teasing, just out of eye's reach.
Sunsets they turn the color of red ochre

mixed with manganese, powdered and blown
through reeds by the early cave painters, fearful
of beasts, to glitter from a bison's frame;

I don't know the exact shade of red-purple
the Phoenicians used to dye robes for kings,
but I think this was it, also the color

of a rose Yeats set afire to see its ghost.
In my mind the ancient Egyptian
who painted amulets inside a royal tomb

wished only for this sizzling fuchsia
to wake the beloved dead, as he mixed gypsum
with rose madder in futile passion.

Once as a child I wandered in the park
bordering my usual asphalt streets,
and saw a flower, red-purple on a stem

with wings. I called to it, my angel.
Now I give an orchid air and water,
turn down the lumière, stroke the crooked stem

that darts out to reveal wings whose vermilion,
burning against a window facing brick,
defies endings on this cold year's end.

Happiness

is not a campfire
but an occulting light,
a field of fireflies
that blink on-off-on,

the tree you planted
whose apples
fall to the ground
half rotten, half sweet,

the street's jackhammers
that fall quiet at night,
the black skimmer's
white underside,

the life together,
apart, together,
the long marriage,
oxymoronic

in its dank joy.
Under a half-moon
quivering
through sycamores,

you held my body
half the night
as I lay in your arms,
sometimes half-awake,

speculating, well,
happy families are unalike.
I choose you
with your handicap,

your half-mobility,
not to mention
your leisure
in forsaking all others

for the chance
of our wholeness.
I take you,
my choice as certain

as plankton on sand
lights up
and arcs to the stars.

The Sand Dancers

In a faded photo, they dance on shore,
two kids we were, scuffing up bursts of sand;
hands rise and fall in a rapid step-slide-spin
on bumpy sand hills, seawater creeping closer.

They shimmy, high as gulls on one another
yet unaware they're skipping on a grave:
the black skull, once a horseshoe crab,
the jellyfish with blood-red intestines,

barnacles stuck fast on eyeless stones
nodding at them like beheaded saints,
seaweed like green hair rising in terror,
commemorate the shipwrecked off this coast,

voyagers and whalers, catch-fishermen.
Now the dancers join hands and swing out,
moonwalk on rocks sea-polished into eggs.
Fresh as sea foam, bright as the break and shuffle

of a long wave gone white before it roars,
its turbulence their only orchestra,
how could they know the years would bring
losses, wars, together, apart, together?

Now it's heel-toe, as if they didn't hear
the clink of a buoy warning of danger
as the chill wind lifts a wave's underbelly
to gather force and strike, all in its time.

Fragments of a Marriage

Fifty-seven years. Your low-rise sports car.
Your plaid necktie slung over a tweed shoulder.
Your visor cap, your pipe, a *meerschaum*,

soapy white, hand carved. My scarf, billowing
as we climbed mountain stairs on Hydra.
Your dive from craggy rocks into the Aegean.

The fountain where we met, playing guitars.
Wimoweh. One world. Faces that blurred until
your green eyes creased in corners when you laughed.

And afterwards, the miracle of ordinariness,
the blue wonder of what we'd known before;
sunlight that picked up stains in stainless flatware.

Your well-deep voice that called for decaf coffee.
Dancing soft-shoe to Mahler, listening
in a storm to a storm of timpani.

Bucking winds that augured an icy winter.
Rolling in waves' foam at the shore's edge.
Waking to the fragrance of Russian sage.

Drafts of our lives. Flaming red-orange-yellow
sketches with no overall design,
brushstrokes waiting for a master's hand.

The finished painting that I knew
we'd never own when you lay perfect, complete.

The Rooted Bed

When the medics lifted your lean body
that once loped over hot sand to the sea,
I wanted them to keep you on our bed

resembling one that waited for Odysseus.
He'd carved the bedpost from an olive tree,
alive, still rooted to the earth. For ours,

you'd found a board cut from an oak
and sanded it until it shone like wheat,
a platform for the mattress, unobtrusive

under a quilt, yet there, your handiwork.
In sickness you lay on the rooted bed.
It never moved, just as we stayed put

in one apartment, and heard things rise:
Schubert's Impromptus on a stereo
you'd built, rooted with electric wires

and plugs to be immovable as well,
a pigeon that chirred on the high sill
(you called it a rock dove), until it flew,

Grand Illusion on a video played
over until we memorized the lines.
The bed is still in place. At night without you

I feel it quiver to put down new roots.

Meteor

That night the wind-chapped table shouted, *new*:
peaches, bread, still warm, and consecrated
by watery breezes on the shore

of a town whose very name, Springs,
was a carillon that jangled newness.
Talking of ancient ruins with my new friends,

I allowed the wind to rinse regrets,
lights winking miles across the bay,
noiseless, but for the surge of waves,

altar-white, before my feet in sand.
And when we turned off lanterns to look skyward
for the Perseids (it was meteor season),

a comet rode queenly across the sky
before it curved and fell. Seeing myself
a speck in the firmament, I remembered

that rock may burn suddenly, blaze into flame
and spin for centuries before it shines
wanting to be remade. Gray rock. The same

that sparkles with mica flecks by day
when breakers slap it clean. Nothing is new.
Nothing alive cannot be altered.

Gone

Washington Square, 2020

From my window, I see the world
without us in it: a vacant park,
a silver maple sheltering no reader;

a cherry tree dressed like a bride betrayed,
her wedding cancelled; a dogwood tree
whose whites will fall without regretful eyes.

No baby strollers; no candy wrappers
stuffed in bins; just a sign, NO BICYCLES,
and memories of skateboard pirouettes.

Around us, death: the numbers spin the mind.
Fever dreams. The last breath held, alone.
I had not thought death had undone so many.

This park reminds us it was once a field
for the unclaimed dead of galloping yellow fever.
Construction workers dug up skeletons

that had lain for years beneath our footsteps.
Death in the hanging elm, a rooted gallows.
Now the clear air, pollution-free, is poison

for walkers, while trees stand stern, immune.
Sad paradox. For comfort, I recall:
Camille Pissarro would have lingered here.

He painted Paris gardens from a window,
having left his island's sprawling shores
for tighter scenes. He gazed at people,

matchsticks from above, in ones and twos.
Below, the park's unlittered paths are mute,
but wait: just now a mournful, prayerful sax,

unseen, from somewhere, unlooses notes,
calls me to the window, and I hear
the sounds I can't imagine days without.

Because

Because, in a wounded universe, the tufts
of grass still glisten, the first daffodil
shoots up through ice-melt, and a red-tailed hawk

perches on a cathedral spire; and because
children toss a fire-red ball in the yard
where a schoolhouse facade was scarred by vandals,

and joggers still circle a dry reservoir;
because a rainbow flaunts its painted ribbons
and slips them somewhere underneath the earth;

because in a smoky bar the trombone blares
louder than street sirens, because those
who can no longer speak of pain are singing;

and when on this wide meadow in the park
a full moon still outshines the city lights,
and on returning home, below the North Star,

I see new bricks-and-glass where the Towers fell;
and I remember my love's calloused hand
soften in my hand while crab apple blossoms

showered our laps, and a yellow rose
opened with its satellites of orange buds;
because I cannot lose the injured world

without losing the world, I'll have to praise it.

Image Worship

Faces on the lid of the Knabe Grand
caught my eye when I tried "The Happy Farmer,"

dreaming of ploughs far from my rutted sidewalks.
Digging, not earth but notes, and neither happy

nor a farmer, I hit wrong keys,
taunted by the metronome. As a distraction,

I stared at smiles in silver frames. War dead.
I never knew them. Heavy-fingered, longing

for their lightness, I saw an uncle waving;
somebody's hell-raiser climbing an oak;

an aunt, a doctor, silk scarf blown in wind.
Suddenly my face appeared among the faces

soon to hide or be interred. The woman's
deep-set eyes in the black-white photograph,

mine in the frame glass, merged, until
the wind lifting her scarf blew through me.

Now, when I stir to brighter images—
a yellow coat, a fawn's sleek arabesque—

I think of photographs, and of Aeneas,
who, in a strange city, stunned by a shrine

with pictures of his own city's destruction,
broken statues, fires, the dead, cried out:

sunt lacrimae rerum: there are tears in things.

Eve Speaks

After you had named *leviathan*,
ziz for great bird, and called out *dissension*
for when the moon glowered at the sun;
creation for beginning, and *expulsion*

for the end, after you gave us *willow*,
thought up *oryx*, and what you tagged *tornado*
sent the olive, God's tree, trembling,
and after symbols—*almonds* for first love,

crocus for lamp glow—you fell silent,
because when you had found labels for *sin*,
archangels, heaven, even (God help you) *God*,
and each new phrase drowned in lion's roar

(or was it divine rage?), you declared *Enough*,
knowing you'd gone too far. Words can't give life
or raise the moon. And still I plead
Say my name, Eve. Say love. Say . . .

Francesca Redux

That day we read no further.

In the beginning, there was the book:
the type, the smell of glue, the grainy paper,
fingertips caressing a stiff spine

that lay flat, the leather cover
crinkled like warm arms, pages fanning open,
stanzas quivering in candlelight,

nouns with open vowels that slid off the tongue,
the wait, the unending sentence with pleasure
delayed. Book, whirl us in wind,

mysterious as marriage, joining words
that had lain apart. After the daily
hoarse falsetto of an alarm clock,

cracked wineglasses and bickering neighbors,
we'll read at night, holding the gilt-edged leaves,
the texts, the bindings that enfold us.

After All

What is it like? You study a hydrangea
that glows lace-white then mauve, and count the whorls
in an oak's huge trunk, split by a hurricane.

You soar with a hawk, not wishing you could fly,
and clamber on the walk in sudden joy.
You linger, seldom glancing at your watch.

You walk to the Hudson River at dawn,
watching a terrier grow out of fog,
and tawny-red bricks that had been blurs

of townhouses the days when you'd whizzed past.
You gaze at them in your own
three-dimensional fullness, unbound,

and you feed the self that you had long neglected
for other selves, the one that knows you best,
and watch the soul burst into sudden bloom,

magenta, like azaleas, and grow larger
when the body lessens.

Light in Genoa

Irma Brandeis, my teacher at Bard

1

Some things come clear only in purest light,
in Montale's Italy, near Genoa,
where the altering sea shimmers at moonrise.

I thought I knew her at the hilltop college,
her black hair clasped like ecstasy held back,
often alone; on walks, she'd name the trees,

asking an oak unanswerable questions.
Green eyes shone sapphire when she spoke of Dante's
doomed lovers, circling on the wind.

I never guessed that she was one of them.
But here, gasping at a fresco's angels,
with sidelong glances that invite the soul,

and at erotic sculptures in a cemetery—
(if the dead could speak, they'd moan in passion)
I imagined a rose in her unbound hair.

2

I knew they had been lovers from his poems
that ring of bellflowers quivering in wind,
phallic cypresses—and there she is,

his Beatrice of the journey that ironically
brought her to Italy. Seeking Dante's hell
she met Montale, thought his humor dull,

his face unfortunate—but not his lines.
So it began, their fire: an incandescent
light at sunset; a balcony in Genoa;

a rocky path, its stones set like mosaics;
swims in a cove. Five years. Then came the shouts
that shattered speech, when shutters slammed

and eyes shut in the sea town's ochre houses.
Nineteen thirty-eight. The Fascist laws.
She left, and just in time. She was a Jew.

3

Montale, hear me now. Life, you once wrote,
is watching a stone wall with cracked glass slivers
stuck on top. One day I stumbled on

a wall like that, high on a mountain terrace,
and knew that you could never risk the climb—
or join her, leaving these gold hours.

Instead, you sent remorse, and married one
who swore suicide if you kept your Clizia,
as you called her, for the water nymph

turned sunflower to watch Apollo,
the sun god whom she loved, in vain. And Clizia
turned into Irma, sunflower to moonflower,

in tailored suits. She never spoke of you.
Only in Genoa, I've understood
that through smart bombs and misery you'd seen her

the way this fire lily breaks through rock
at the sea's edge, in the unfractured light
that is, perhaps, the hero of your story.

Moment in Rapallo

Your mind went double, like these two brass doorknobs
that lead into your house. I tried one. Locked.
Years past you had unlocked my mind to hear

language charged with meaning, and to feel
that sense of sudden growth, and as for rhythm,
the churn, the loom,

                the spinning wheel, the oar.

An old scribe quotes King Solomon:
God created our organs in duplicate,
two hearts, two minds.

                For you, two loyalties.

No pure homage, then, these lines go double
for the mind that battened on division
as it winced and stirred:

                I pictured you

descending from your attic to the harbor
where triangle sails fishermen call lateens
called back ancient boats,

                the past made new.

There you were, in your seaside caffè,
listening to wave-sounds while declaiming
in two languages;

                arranging concerts

for your double-love, a violinist
playing Bach in praise beyond division.
I'd seen you that way.

        But now, suddenly,

my hand on an unyielding yellow doorknob,
fiery through the mist, after a storm
had sunk harbor boats

        like your once-buoyant

mind, capsized, split, at once I see:
the fascist salute; the love turned sour;
the right turned wrong,

        the *language charged*

with meaning suddenly meaningless, degraded,
madness denied at first, the mind's locked door.
I pulled my hand back,

        fearing the brass might,

as in gilt statues, rub off in my palm.

Alive and Well: Tomb Sculptures in the Staglieno Cemetery

Genoa, Italy

1 ANGEL

So this is death, lifelike in marble
and unconsoling, on a merchant's tomb.
No man with a scythe, no man at all,
but her, slim-hipped in an airy gown

nipped at the waist; on the high breast
one hand rests, the slender fingers
limp, waiting to beckon or direct,
come-hither lips—barbed wings.

The eyes translucent, clear lakes
you want to fathom, but the gaze
says, I don't want to be known
or understood. Angel of cold passion.

Angel of sex and death: essential answers
hidden in one vamp. When I pass by,
she turns to follow. Death, you terrify—
just as you lure me with a knowing glance.

2 WIDOW

I know her by the pleated satin dress,
hair in a bun, the hesitation
as she lifts the sheet, letting air in,
astonished, peering into darkness—

(what will she find there?)—at her husband's body,
suddenly altered. Questions run through her:
dare she kiss the lips now growing colder?
Can he hear her? Leaning awkwardly,

loath to leave him, venturing a touch,
she asks now, why him? In unending silence,
she clings to precise details for an answer,
side-glancing at the unmade bed, the high

pile of cushions falling from their place.
I know her by my husband's silver watch
that hasn't stopped. The still warm belly.
The pearl pajama button on the terrace.

3   DREAMER

Clerics opposed her installation here,
so close to rosaries, hands clasped in prayer.
Officials said: a travesty of holiness,
pagan, impious. Other slurs unclear.

What was it? Not the lips about to part,
the mouth to speak, the tousled hair,
the robe that slides down a bare shoulder,
curvy hips—those were the sculptor's art.

Nor was it her calm perch, dreaming, not dead.
The dream, though: those three ovals in her hand,
seemingly blossoms, are poppy pods
formed after flowering, from whose sticky substance

opium is drawn. Demeter in grief
over her daughter's fate, would sip the stuff
to soothe her loss. At the Staglieno,
sexy is fine. Is life. Addiction, no.

4   MARIA FRANCESCA

Eyes shut, as in elation more than death,
the legs straining to spring from their marble bed,
a sheet slipped to reveal the nude young breasts,
spool waist. Not the shattered body found

in a car crash, fingers severed and flung,
this likeness is perfect, shaped, from a photograph
—notice the glow, the urge to speak, to laugh.
Unlike some broken statues, hinting at arms

and phalluses, she gleams in all her parts.
Alone but not alone. Her man in marble
bends to kiss her and clutch her thigh,
not in lust but in finality.

I know the scene. Your body fixed but yearning
to move again. I'm moving now in scattered
pieces, over miles and time. Free neither
to finish the task of life nor to abandon it.

5   STRUGGLE

If these stones were flesh, you'd hear their cries:
Death, blank-faced and stiff, and a lithe woman
who won't be taken by those tigery claws
without a kick, a blow, a fierce objection.

She bends, covered waist down in see-through tulle,
actually marble carved to look ethereal
with the same mallet, calipers, and chisel
the sculptor used to shape rock into muscle.

Waist up exposed, but raging, unafraid.
The work unfinished, dinners to order,

dresses to try on, letters to write.
When, that last night, you called for slacks and blazer
from your sickbed, I watched the pull-away,
the savage, sun-driven though futile, fight.

6 WOMAN IN SUNLIGHT

Carved in marble, white now gone to grime,
mottled, soot-blotched, smeared, with blurred letters,
a lithe woman reclines in a gauzy nightdress,
curved from substantial hip to supple ankles,

but for the cross she holds, I'd say in languor.
Stare at her, stare until you see lean hands
open to grasp at air, feet kick to dance,
silk hair unfold like a billowing scarf,

and linger for the long intake of breath.
I want to move inside the blackened stone
and find a spark that flares up into blaze

and flashes like sunbeams—to dazzle
with tales of what it could be like to walk
out of my weathered body. Clean. Alive.

Ascension

That morning, in the Church of the Ascension
on lower Fifth, once a sanctuary
for bonnets and top hats, I had a vision

of clipped pines, bamboo, a Kyoto garden.
Odd. In La Farge's painting above the altar,
Christ rises from the dead while his disciples

gaze heavenward, and angels swim in air,
two and two and two, draped in white silk.
But why bamboo? Perhaps I had a reason.

La Farge, his marriage ended, brushes dry,
went to Japan and gasped when he found Fuji.
He saw the mountaintop float like a god,

loom over him, and fade. At once renewed,
he painted Christ rising from the hills
to heaven's kingdom. And when I looked

long enough, the Mount of Olives
changed into Mount Fuji's snowcapped cone,
immobile, while a stream flows, an image

of what Lao Tsu called life's stillness and motion.
Now, in the Church of the Ascension,
I praise all things that soar and make a crowd

glance skyward: a wave of white thistledown,
an egret's dangling legs in flight; a siren-red
balloon; snow wafting high; a Buddhist's moon;

La Farge's Christ that turns into the Great Buddha
shimmering in bronze; and after that
Mohammed's horse; Elijah's chariot

let fly above the altar. I'll be there,
gazing impiously—unless
that is what sacred is, the work, the looking up,
                              the wonder.

Agony in the Garden

*Oil on canvas, Giovanni Bellini,
National Gallery, London*

No garden,   not
in the leafy sense.

No Eden,   certainly,
just high treeless rock.

See me now,   no god,
a man, afraid.   Friends,

or so they swore, loved as they
could. Now   I'm hunted,

they fake sleep. How can I—
can I run from

betrayal?   Is this a cup
of poison   or salvation?

A prickly   altar for prayer:
granite with   knifeblade edges,

and here's no   ordinary
first light. Clouds' underbellies,

silver at dawn,   bode lightning.
Or a shock   of angels.

Tell me which   it will be.
Pray for them   pray

for stillness,   pray
to do right.

My sweat runs red
freely,   like blood

streaming,   thigh gashed
on a razory rock.

Look there,   far away,
flies swarming in sight?

No, soldiers wandering
over a bridge,   at ease,

harmless.   Almost
restful.   At rest.

At last.
Arrest.

That Summer

Joy began with a cerulean sky
and breaths of grass, sweeter than subway odors.
My mind was playing over the warm hard runs

of Sonny Rollins on tenor sax,
in rhythm with the roll of a wooden pier,
brash kids beside me, gleaming wet in sun.

Urgent yet serene, his tones kept hidden
what I'd read of his early addiction.
Crime, jail. Overcome. No lasting harm.

Lifted, perhaps, by someone's sturdy arms.
Savoring the single notes and lulls,
risking the wild delight of his "Gazelle,"

I knifed into the lake, seemingly tranquil,
limpid, with emerald weeds. A sudden whirl
pulled me around. I swam, steering upward,

and turned—the wrong way. Blue pain. My head
hit the deck's underside, no space to breathe.
I thought the tide would suck me down to mud.

No, someone saw. Sturdy arms dragged me up,
changed, knowing how close bliss was to dread
and how it must have been to yell for help,

hear no sound, and scream through your horn instead.

The Vow

That day I stepped gingerly with my father
playing father (actors played their parts)
down the blue-carpeted aisle to be wed

—or tried for treason. A skeletal pianist
fingered a funeral march, hitting wrong notes.
We passed Mom in a dress sizes too large

she'd bought to play the mother-of-the-bride.
My own tight bodice pinched as I gasped for breath,
bound for a new life, knowing the old would do.

I glanced upward at friends playing hope,
my roses drying brown as I neared an altar
set too high and built of rotting pine.

My father gave this woman, me, to some
imposter who would want me to be faithful
as Ruth, which meant, I supposed, to follow

my mother-in-law, whither she goest.
Yes, I wanted this, but want is a moment
in a long sentence without punctuation.

What if like some birds I could not sing
in captivity? Would it be, I pleaded,
security or maximum security?

Divorce would disappoint my grandmother
crying here (for joy?) in silk chiffon.
And then at last I saw him, the one

who wasn't playing anyone, his eyes
hazel, shining like aggies in first light—
and I said *yes, of course, I will, I will.*

Cinderella

I was fifteen, too thin, and six feet tall
with outsize feet, though still believing
in a glass slipper. Until that night

at a high school dance, when the teacher barked,
*Every girl must toss one shoe on the mound
for a boy to choose and take its owner.*

I gazed at shells in suede, in patent leather,
swirly, with curvy insteps, ice pick heels,
and tucked my flat-heeled sandal under them,

nails clawing through the heel I'd hammered off
to stand a half-inch lower. They had said
someday you'll be glad you're tall. But someday

was tonight. I hoped that some odd suitor
would see beyond the shoe to me myself.
Boys hunted the heap. I saw my sandal

left alone, intruder in the ring
before the teacher poked it with a pointer,
watched it squirm, and hoisted it high:

Whose shoe is this? No need to ask again.
I ran home barefoot in the rain, skidding
on slick pavement, resolved to find my way
that night and after. Never mind the prince.

Dr. John

Stage name of Malcolm John Rebennack, Jr.

Remember strutting high in the night air
at Mardi Gras. Wearing the Voodoo gown,
silky emerald, bones and crosses clinking,

hands racing on keys. Remember losing
the beat. Losing time, and time was all,
like watching your shadow fade at dusk.

Trying to call down the beat, *Shallow water,
yo ma-ma, hu-tunnay two-way pock-a-way,*
accents weak as a rain chant in a storm

outshouted by thunder, pleas unheard.
Drinking cure-alls with jimson weed, stroking
embroidered amulets, scrapping your name,

Rebennack, for Dr. John, a caster of spells
who wielded snakes. Invoking Voodoo queens,
lifting the doll, rubbing the healing stone,

and when the charms failed, drugs, jail,
where you watched days merge in mist, out of time,
eyes blurred, unfocused. Now from a high window

in the detox ward, you see a woodchuck waddle
then run to miss car wheels. Turning back,
you eye the lock box, drugs, dreams inside.

To pry it open would mean jail again.
*Gonna take my gang on Mardi Gras day,
say mighty coody-fiyo get out of the way.*

Half notes pound. You lie back in bed
and twitch awake, under a hawk's claw
on a low flight, blackjack, handcuffs, the law.

No talons. Instead, a woman's hand, an orderly's:
tapered fingers open on a ball,
saggy, pocked skin, color of sunset.

You bite into a tangerine, unpeeled,
and feel sweet-sour trickle down your throat.
Cool dawn. Then fire, as when you heard the beat

that first day in your father's music store,
and went out under stars, singing, *Yo-mama,
hu-tunnay two-way pock-a way.*

It was good. And on another Sunday
in a crowded ward, you heard the beat.

The Rainbow Sign

*God gave Noah the rainbow sign,
No more water, the fire next time.*

Like cotton candy, spun of cloud and air,
two ribbons slipped from yardage under the earth
spooling out brightness past a sea of shipwrecks.

Yesterday's hurricane spun through the village,
shattering panes, burying cars in sand,
splintering a neighbor's wooden pier,

its piles still jutting up like broken molars,
wrenching wires, screaming of loss.
Blackout. Our faces flushed in candlelight,

we watched nerve-ends of lightning shock the windows
and questioned wall shadows for predictions.
Today, the rainbow sign, God's weather news:

*The waters shall never again become a flood
to destroy all flesh.*
                        Relief? Well, promises,
the longing for belief that comes in language

clear as in a child's coloring book:
violet, blue, green, yellow, orange, red,
upgraded here to lilac, cobalt, clay,

new life green, wheat yellow, and carmine.
Rainbow, heal the world with sudden light.
Let us drive into bars of tinted gauze

then hide indoors until the fire next time.

Caregiver

Caretaker, career
                steward, sworn lover,

companion, recorder
                of heart rates, if heart

can be rated;
                unresting, reminder

of amethyst hours.
                Carrier of cheer,

custodian of someone
                no one can own;

head manager, planner,
                quick to the answer,

unfazed, of the phone,
                never alone—

stitched to the other,
                a secret sharer,

and, like the sinner
                condemned to a circle

of howlers in hell,
                hearing one call.

Survival in the Woods

1

After the chapel prayers, I went to the woods
for clearance, clearings in trees, clearness
of mind. For sunlight on the ground
strained through leaves. Dazed by loss,

I came for images of things that last:
catbrier that hooks tendrils into bark.
Poplars that soar unbroken, hushed in rain,
and high-branched oaks, wind's roarers

that toss their topmost leaves like dice
in a game of chance, taking the odds on danger.
The Baal Shem Tov, carrying sorrow
for those in pain, built fires in the woods,
sat balanced on a splintered log, and when
prayer didn't come, he'd tell a story.

2

On this land the colonists thought Satan,
masked as a Mohawk, lurked among the maples,
so Satan hurled dank images at me:
white grubs, possums, blind worms, and, slimier,

water snakes from under the brown leaf carpet,
star-nosed moles, onyx-and-purple slugs,
all crawlers. As I stared they glittered
in the dark woods, and I remembered brightness.

Once I'd misread a museum plaque, Pissarro's
"Edge of the Woods" for "Edge of the World."
He'd left wide shores to paint tight woods in France,

finding new freedom in limitation.
At the world's edge, slender vines cling
to ancient alders. Life holds on to life.

3

Oaks claim their dead. Poets, young suicides,
are here grown into pines. But claiming life,
Jews lived in the woods, evading guards,
crouched in holes, starved, drinking from rivers.

A branch snaps. I remember my origin,
not as I had thought, in my tall city
of sidewalk squares, but in the forest
where new shoots break through dry-leaf cover,

where there are no full-stops, only motion
that leads me on, where the trail before me
slopes to blankness, and I land unharmed.
My name is Schulman, mine by a long marriage,
though I had another name at birth:
Waldman, woodman, survivor in the woods.

From The Letting Go

1 WAITING MUSIC

Evenings I watch the junipers turn gray
waiting for the peppermill grind
of your key in the lock, the door's groan,
the arrow of light, the spin of leaves, your car

crunch gravel and light up the ivy
you'd sunk in earth. Spring, when the garden's flush
with gold—dandelion, buttercup—the finch
taunts, dead means dead, not just away

investigating dendritic cells
to cure diseases. Your Bach CD stalls
downtempo. I grow older. Hear my plea.
Had you sailed the river in a storm
I'd have worn boots and trampled out at dawn
to meet you, as far as Cho-Fu-Sa.

2 THE SECOND LINE

You knew the odds on death, your practiced mind
reeled with the diagnosis, *Cardiac
Failure, Stage Four*. And still you planned
Philharmonic nights, one of them jazz,

whose pair of tickets sears my calendar.
Go, New Orleans jazzmen, hit a low note
for the man who craves your flourishes.
Celebrate. Start up the second line,

trumpet and snare drum. Play it hot, up-tempo.
Let the street crowd amble, strut, kick high.

Open the scarlet petals of umbrellas
and spin with dancers as the band wails.

There you are, foot-tapping. In silver light
you listen to a man in a silk top hat
who shouts: "Rejoice. Another soul gone home."
The saints go marching in to raise a life.

3   REGRET

    After Thomas Wyatt

My schooner filled to brimming with regret
sails in a storm. Breakers flood the deck,
rising slow, in rhythm of deep breaths.
You, radiant as loss, stand at the helm,

clutching the wheel. See, white sails worn brown
with tears of gale-force winds that cracked the engine.
We steer into the eye, all safety gone.
The mind reels with what it can't imagine

of death. Now, limping through rapid currents
between rocks and shale, I dwell on Reason
and Foresight that like trusted tenants
skipped without paying rent, the should-have-done
and might-have-said my torment. Stars blur
tonight as mist consumes the harbor.

4   FIRST CHILL—THEN STUPOR—
THEN THE LETTING GO—

There is no letting go. Your tenor, singing
Bach off-key, still rises to high ceilings.
Hazel eyes, creased at their corners, dazzle
my bathroom mirror. Your midnight blue

brass-button blazer and your lace-up Oxfords,
for opera nights, are waiting in your closet.
Students and friends have anxious looks. I'm here,
hoisting a wheeler bag, holding a passport

for a strange shore, life incomplete.
One morning a high wave will stall to reveal
its cobalt underside, crash on the rock

I hold, and loosen my grip. In the waves' wash,
a leaking dinghy will sail, motorlesss.
I'll climb aboard and try to bail it out.

FROM *Without a Claim* (2013)

Celebration

Seeing, in April, hostas unfurl like arias,
and tulips, white cups inscribed with licks of flame,
gaze feverish, grown almost to my waist,
and the oaks raise new leaves for benediction,
I mourn for what does not come back: the movie theater—
reels spinning out vampire bats, last trains,
the arc of Chaplin's cane, the hidden doorways—
struck down for a fast-food store; your rangy stride;
my shawl of hair; my mother's grand piano.
My mother.

                How to make it new,
how to find the gain in it? Ask the sea
at sunrise how a million sparks
can fly over dead bones.

The Sound

Accabonac, Shinnecock, Peconic, Napeague,
the creek, the bay, the stream, the Sound, the sounds

of consonants, hard c's and k's. Atlantic,
the ocean's surge, the clicks of waves

collapsed on rocks in corrugated waters,
the crowd circling a stranded whale

sent by the god Moshup to beach at Paumanok.
The Montauks left us names. Their successors,

Millers and Bennetts, whose names are carved
on local gravestones, rode rough tides,

strung trawl lines for cod, and even on Sundays
parked vans by the sea and gazed in fear

until commercial hauls replaced their boats.
Surfmen gave names to streets that bag the tourists

who prize their charm. I hear old sailors rage,
in many languages, against cold winds,

the light now clear, now haze: Pharoahs and Mulfords,
whalers (names unknown), hurl throaty curses

that rise with the sound of waves and with the cries
of an ice-colored gull plucking scallops in shallows.

Without a Claim

Raised like a houseplant on a windowsill
looking out on other windowsills
of a treeless block, I couldn't take it in

when told I owned this land with oaks and maples
scattered like crowds on Sundays, and an underground
strung not with pipes but snaky roots that writhed

when my husband sank a rhododendron,
now flaunting pinks high as an attic window.
This land we call our place was never ours.

If it belonged to anyone, it was
the Montauk chief who traded it for mirrors,
knowing it wasn't his. Not the sailors

who brought the blacksmith iron, nor the farmers
who dried salt hay, nor even the later locals,
whale hunters, the harpooner from Sumatra,

the cook from Borneo, who like my ancestors
wandered from town to port without a claim,
their names inside me though not in the registries.

No more than geese in flight, shadowing the lawn,
cries piercing wind, do we possess these fields,
given the title, never the dominion.

But here we are in April, watching earth rise
with bellflowers that toll, brawl, call, in silence;
daffodils that gleam yellow through sea haze

and cedars at sunrise asking for flame
like a cake with tiers of birthday candles.
Come visit us by shore, up a mud lane.

Duck under the elm's branches, thick with leaves,
on land deeded to us but not to keep,
and take my hand, mine only to give

for a day that shines like corn silk in wind.
We rent, borrow, or share even our bodies,
and never own all that we know and love.

Moon Shell

August, I walk this shore in search of wholeness
among snapped razor clams and footless quahogs.
How easily my palm cradles a moon shell

coughed up on shore. I stroke the fragments
as, last night, I stroked your arm
smelling of salt, scrubbed clean by the sea air.

Once you loped near me. Now, in my mind's eye,
your rubbery footsoles track sand hills
the shape of waves you no longer straddle.

You inch forward, step, comma, pause,
your silences the wordless rage of pain.
But still at night our bodies merge in sleep

and fit unbroken, like the one perfect shell
I've never found and can only imagine—
and crack when we're apart. I clutch the moon shell,

guardian of unknowing, chipped and silent,
until I fling it down and feel its loss.
Broken, it fit my hand and I was whole.

Antiques Fair

Tents bloom like the circus over things
that serve new purposes: the family hymnal
drowses in a cradle, mugs offer razors,
gifts of an ancestor who isn't yours.

A woman wearing cloudy froth sorts pewter
and holds a blue bottle to the sunlight,
then strokes a gilded mirror for the image
of an 1890s great-grandmother,

young in a tulle gown, plush stole, and tiara.
Sunday, July. In town, the church is empty.
Stark pulpit. Preacher gone. The organist
in a fair booth squinting at tattered sheet music,

"Rejoice, You Pure," the congregation out
picking at fries, bowed over what might read:
*Blessed art thou, bald eagle in blond wood,
beak agape, swoop down and clutch us now.*

A mother reaches around the baby
strapped on her chest to scoop up beads
marked VINTAGE, V for the vast enchanted
who sleepwalk through the fair, lifting tongs

forged by a local smith, as though to salvage
from a great fire icons of a past
flimsy as a chain of paper dolls,
bare as a brass fist with a missing flagpole.

Hurricane

Warnings go unheard in all this brightness.
Sun's fire licks the poplars on a road
that will be flooded in, they say, three hours.

Abandon homes. Move on, or else you'll spin
with the storm on radar, now an amoeba,
sleeping, one great eye narrowed to an almond,

now a ball of ice tossed in the air,
poised to cast out sharp needles to the ground.
The flagpole trembles on the courthouse roof.

The city gates are closing. Save yourself.
What to believe? On a flat bay, wet wind
washes me clean. Crows are crows, not prophecies.

If so, why does the lightning zigzag closer?
Why are my hands so cold? Because the law
flashes in white letters: *Seek higher ground.*

Why are the people buying Yahrzeit candles
in glass jars, the kind that burn all night?
Because they are the only lights in stores.

Because God, who sends floods, gives us sight,
powerless unpowered. When the marina's
a spectral dock, my body is the only ark

to weather high waves. In screaming darkness,
my neighbor's voice, yesterday a growl,
drifts softly. Now a lamp flickers, now

the storm has passed, the city gates swing open
in a deadly calm. Unpack my fears.
I cannot see the fire in the poplars.

Letter Never Sent

> *I always knew in my heart Whitman's mind to be more like my own than any man's living. As he is a very great scoundrel, this is not a pleasant confession.* — Gerard Manley Hopkins

Bawd, savage, unbeliever,
my enemy my brother,
sloucher in the picture

I turn from, wanderer
in and out of the game,
your *heart in hiding,*

your hope flares with the osprey
on serrated wings.
I have learned to say

sassafras, black walnut,
beech, as in your country,
and know as you do

the wren's inscape,
God's mystery stressed,
instressed. You speak

holier than I know
with your *signatures*
and your *handkerchief of the Lord;*

your dogwood, my white beam,
the cross that belongs
to neither, and is ours.

How you see the self
inside the ash;
your *Leaves of Grass*

cling like my Sybil's leaves
blown about her cave,
both as infinite

as *the journeywork of the stars.*
Keep my hayfields. They are yours:
your runs and flourishes, mine.

Let each in his way
catch the hawk alive in air,
tongue-tied, stammering,

in whatever whirled words
will suffice.
I've memorized six of your poems

and must not go further.
The more desirous to read you,
the more determined

I will not,
for my eyes lift to Heaven,
not simply the heavens

of puffed clouds and stars.
Like you I gaze
at masculine trees,

but as you risk
the dangerous beauty
of a boy's bare waist,

I love and fear my love
for the perfect shoulder
of Christ: I see it now,

neck curls, forked beard,
stiff crucified arms
that brought me to Him.

And though I have dreamed
of strolling barefoot
in a green park,

caught my portrait
in a spoon's mirror,
and gazed at Leonardo's bodies,

we cannot walk together,
I in black soutane, you
in an open shirt,

nor can I send this letter,
Jesuit to scoundrel,
unconverted.

Still, in the fire at dawn,
and in the sea's whorls,
mind to mind,

God to God,
Walt to Gerard,
I hear your voice.

Street Music, Astor Place

There he is, outside the subway entrance
where sunlit figures race down steps to darkness,
their hearing, like mine, dulled by traffic whines.

He sits low and drums jazz on a plastic box,
turned upside down, white with blue letters
stamped by its owner, U.S. POSTAL SERVICE,

made for mail, though with an alto's range.
Now he raises sticks and beats staccato
up-tempo, faster than your foot can tap.

Judging from his gaze, the eyes unfocused
— no money jug in sight, no pause for offerings,
no violin cases open like birds' beaks —

I'd say he dives for notes that only he hears,
and swims up proud. He raps sticks soft and loud,
alone, though he may think his rattling joins

a trumpeter's phrases blown at breakneck speed
or a pianist's feathery arpeggios.
For me it does: the sound calls back a cave

of smoke, talk, laughter. A bass player solos.
A tenor sax eases out notes in a whisper
that grows into a regal tone and floats

above the chords. Faces gleam at tables.
But no, the subway-entrance man's alone.
He rumbles on, catching the city's breath,

rolling out solitude in the midst of clatter.
His playing says, if you rub two sticks together
you'll have fire. Or, you might have music.

Woman on the Ceiling

Dura-Europos Synagogue, 245 C. E.

Her face shines from the ceiling, ample hair
unbound, the color of wheat in wind,
leaves caught in its stray wisps, her skin paler

than the dark hands of congregants below
reaching to touch the Law on silver scrolls
shouldered and hoisted high from a plaster niche.

She rises shyly, questioning, eyes wide
in this narrow synagogue, the elders
innocent of how the second commandment

will be invoked one day: no graven images.
Who are you, nameless beauty? How you glow
near other bright depictions: a sea monster,

ripe grapes, a lusty goat. To your painter,
you might be just another Aphrodite,
topless and seductive, luring celebrants

to the pagan temple down the path,
or a match for saints in the city church
that face front and stare with the same moon eyes.

Your viewers cannot hear the threats, the bans,
the don'ts that came later: don't look up,
don't ever think about the face of Eve

or Adam's thighs in sensuous brushstrokes
on a chapel ceiling. No, keep the law.
You were there all the time, buried in sand,

when artists were artisans, makers of objects,

a silver Kiddush cup, a candleabrum,
unmindful of the breeze twirling your hair.

Now stumbling over rocks in the third century,
the synagogue whole again, just as it was,
I hear the words, *how manifold thy works*,

chanted by congregants whose lifted eyes
see beyond you, through gaps in the wall,
to desert plain, imagining date palms.

You were there all the time, sister of saints
and goddesses, hauled up with shards of a jar,
lost coins, the puzzle of a child's shoe,

a helmet and a sword belt for protection
against attacks, and a gold ring engraved
with only one word, *homonoia*. Unity.

My Father's Watches

Antiques, they tick
for weeks after winding.

When wound they wound me
into wondering

how those faint bells
can tune up when I pass,

and faces stare, wide-eyed,
silver moons tooled with angels,

hunters, and satyrs.
Don't steal my time,

he didn't say, his look rebuking
only himself. He seldom rested

but for the hours
he polished his congregation

of watches, hearing the beat,
gazing at fixed stars.

They kept his days whole
in a blur of motion

even on Sundays at home,
when he brought us smoked fish,

inhaled it like perfume,
and arranged a palette of red-white

slices on a platter,
then combed files of letters

from his parents in Poland,
hoping they were still alive.

Once, while seconds spun,
he listened to a poem

that had come to me slowly.
He glanced at his pocket moon,

and when he turned away
I could see that no words

could mute the drone
of planes in his head.

Watches, give me time
to write lines

my father might hear
over bombs and gunfire.

Havdalah

Braided candle, a rainbow of colored wax
twists upward in this sea house. I remember
Saturdays when three stars dotted the sky

candlelight ended Sabbath, red, blue, yellow
casting black silhouettes on plaster walls.
Clutching wine in a silver cup, my father

led us in a chant to praise division
of holy day from weekday, light from shadow.
Sundays my father braided my taffy hair

into one rope over my middy collar
while singing in a half-forgotten Polish,
and now I look at waves and see the basket weavers

of the Montauk people who lived here,
women plaiting swamp grass and flat reeds,
farmers binding wheat, the carder and the twiner,

hand over hand, all workers looking down
at wheat or loom or treebark in the same way.
Tonight, at Sabbath's end, in this seaside town

far from my first house, new faces glow
in the three-color fire of a braided candle,
all of them guests, like me, and the flame

tells me that havdalah, meaning separation,
divides only to join. Candle, you light
my hands in altering jade and sapphire,

and braid colors together, silk thread
woven into the billowing fire-red tunic
in Castagno's portrait of a Florentine,

yellow for the luminous medallion
in a Muslim prayer rug, the gold thread
in a carpet hung to warm a castle's walls,

the silver in a chapel's blue-green tapestry
and here, footprints in sand where fishermen
in wine-red shirts braid ropes tight as your coils.

Charles Street Psalm

Downtown, where towers redden after sunrise,
I heard the singing, more like sobbing, harsh,
broken measures, out of tune, choked sighs,
pour from a brick synagogue set between townhouses,

unadorned and hardly noticeable
but not unnoticing: one immense window,
unblinking in the sun-on-river glare,
looked back at me coldly as I looked in.

I did not know the words, but I caught tremolos
of praise; thanksgiving, oddly, in lament,
blessings grief undivided. I counted twelve,
but I heard thousands, ancestors whose voices

traveled over theirs, amassed in one
common wail, like wind gusts over seas.
Pesukei d'Zimrah, morning praise,
each day a psalm sung now, sung then by exiles

in a past my father blurred with Chardonnay.
He seldom spoke of old world, of horse wagons
that jostled him, in hiding, from the road
where his brother, Jan, was shot, nor of his pack

that held Jan's poems which he declaimed for coins,
a grease-stained photo, newspapers to line
freezing shoes. He told another story:
one morning, after fogbound days on shipboard,

caught in the mystery of what would come,
he saw the harbor. Stream spurted from rock,
garnets in sunlight. He thanked brick towers,
sheltered, as I would be, as *they* would be—

twelve early risers on Charles Street—
where the only soldier-and-rifle shadows
were cast by ginkgo and redbud trees,
where the river exploded only with sunrays,

and where the truck that zigzagged over cobblestones
carried only stacked cartons of milk.
Still, those gravelly, unaccompanied
baritones chanted my father's dread-

and-joy that lurked in his discarded memories.
The past he tucked under damask napkins:
one-room house, dirt road on moonless nights,
comes back to me whole. First breath. Possibilities.

Walking to Elijah

She loomed before me like a prophecy,
wearing a black robe that swept the sand
and a dangling crucifix. I stared until

her eyes beamed under a birdlike crest.
She had observed me through the chapel window,
carrying poppies, a worn map, and a note

with ink-blurred numbers, home of my hosts
for Sabbath dinner, 17 Elijah.
The sun went down, squeezed like a fat stewed peach

too bulky for its jar. It would soon be dark.
Her coarse sleeve grazed my arm as she held torn paper.
"I don't know the address, but we'll walk together.

It's good gymnastics." Gliding in black folds
(I thought she'd fly) she waved the scrap
at a man sipping tea. "There's no such place,"

he barked. "Yes, there must be, she's lost her way,"
my black angel insisted, and he joined us.
Lost. Yesterday a bomb had exploded here

responding to arrests. Shops closed. And now
the Sabbath, day of rest, its supplications
for peace unheeded. Soon our group was growing

into a procession. Asked for Elijah Street,
passersby shrugged and fell in. One lean man
offered advice in Serbian; at the next corner,

a woman stood sobbing, until, curious,
she crept along. People followed me—
or was I following them? Where were we headed?

We passed a mosque, a church in ruins, a cloister.
Hats were skullcaps, knitted cartwheels, scarves,
a fez, over faces with family features.

Inside a basement window, men at prayer
gazed upward: a black condor? No, the nun.
She hovered, then made for another house

and rang a doorbell, the diners sitting down
to Sabbath wine. Still, no one knew Elijah.
It was late before I reached my friends,

and I don't remember anything else that evening
except a black gown, hats, opinions crackling
in a fire of languages that halted prayer.

Hickories

Why do I write of hickories, whose boughs
touch other boughs across a slender road,
when our neighbor, Haneen, born in Gaza,

cried that a missile ripped her niece apart
in the family garden? The child's father
found her intestines stuck to a cypress bark

and he, too, perished in the raid. Her mother
wrote to Haneen before the news was out,
"Help me. Take my hand." Why do I rave

of hickories reaching out their crooked fingers?
Because before the fires, the child, Lina,
was dropping almonds into a linen napkin.

Soon she would run to offer them for dinner.
Like Lina, I race to show you hickories,
their nuts shrunken brown globes, soon to fall.

Shadow

Once in Paris I heard a woman sing
of a day to come so hot that sunrise
would dry the seas, the only sound on earth

a cricket's drone, and on that day,
I search for your heart as I search for shadow.
She sang, looked up at me, coal eyes, pale skin,

and a cool wind poured from the narrow street
into the cave, dissolving smoke and talk.
I didn't know the story: at the time

the singer loved a black American,
a trumpeter, both twenty-two. I see them run
down boulevards, hear blues. The dream

ended when he left, she stayed, knowing
that stares and jeers would dog their steps downtown.
While the chanteuse invoked a new Pigalle,

the trumpeter, alone, cursing in street talk,
blew notes of loss, spun out of air and silence.
And why recall it now? Well, on this day

in a hot July, when the sun wilts maples,
when fireworks glare from land's end every night,
starbursts shooting high, dimming the stars,

when only the ocean breathes, and the radio tells
of slaughter, a jazz trumpeter cuts in,
playing up-tempo, and clears the air.

Yellow

Chris Albertson at Riverside Records

But first, his yellow hair, like sunshot clouds,
the blur of a finch through dark pines,
the suddenness of wheat fields at high noon,

the sherry rose that outgrows its trellis,
the chrome of a Japanese print blazing
in a fisherman's coat painted by Van Gogh,

color of memory, color of angels,
and the surprise of it, as though
the Danish lakes had washed out all impurities,

not like mine, whose ancestors must have waded
muddier waters. When Chris spoke, I saw North,
fjords and mussel beds on coasts

where he spun a rod fishing for trout.
He told me he left Denmark for the South.
Early, he stirred to jazz LPs, to Bessie's

murmurs he would cross an ocean for.
On trains, on foot, he taped field hollers, blues,
work songs, to cut recordings in New York;

ambushed a tenor sax cleaning a washroom;
amazed a bass who hauled bags at the train;
raised up a blind beggar moaning "Search My Soul"

on a rain-wracked guitar. Found Ida Cox,
old, still in good voice, who would record
"Hard, Lord," her bent notes filled with pain

risen in praise. What had brought him there?
Yellow again. Yellow of a wartime childhood.
Yellow stars on badges Denmark's Jews

were forced to wear. The king pinned one on.
Dane citizens. His father. Shadows lifted.
North became South, all colors yellow, yellow.

At the Physical Therapist's

You strain for balance on a fat blue globe,
hoping to walk steadily again,

to stand up for the Hallelujah chorus,
kick up autumn leaves, scuff sand, trek anywhere.

I'm told to lurk behind the rubbery planet
crouched to spring if you should quiver and fall.

Pleats of your shirt deepen as you sway
and right yourself again, your shoulders tense,

and you bitch and curse at someone (fate?
the wounding angel?), mourn your lost strides,

squirm in forced stillness. I think of risk,
your risk, and mine as I write this now,

treading a circus wire strung between landings.
eyes fixed on the line ahead, without a pole.

In Praise of Shards

From far away I saw a low curved thing
awash on shore, a corpse, stripped nude and lying

among chipped shells and stones, bone-white at noon,
a woman, one arm outstretched, the other gone,

legs splayed, hacked at the ankle.
But no. Closer, just driftwood, a tall

cedar, branchless, scoured of its stringy bark.
Unlike Aphrodite, leaning in marble,

long fingers lost, hands snapped off over time,
this wood sculpture, carved by an unseen maker

with the turbulent sea for gouge and mallet,
was nameless and *began* with missing parts.

Only the pelvis was intact, skin smooth,
unsplintered by the harsh ride, and hinting

at other wholenesses, inviting me
to imagine the cut extended arm

in prayer, and shape the head to speak or sing.
I came for answers, asking a cracked shell:

Why does the mind reach for completeness
when the fragments are all we have?

My mother's note. I found it in her jewelry case
after she died, "These are real pearls, they . . ."

The rest was blurred. I see her at her table
writing what she could never say without

noticing I had not caught their fire.
The ropes are gone. The image is what stays.

Chauvet

Raise a torch to flicker on cave walls
and see the horses caught in flight, sleek manes
rising like smoke rings in clear air.
Some dark force lured a nomad
to crawl into a cave with a homemade lamp:

his palette, colors of earth, fire, ash,
charcoal from burned pine, and blood red ochre
he'd blow through a reed. He scraped the paint
and rubbed out lines until the last horse reared
and the dream took form: imperious stag,

rhino, bison, aurochs, stories on walls.
What drew him there? Not hunger but the hunger,
when winter threatened, nightfall terrified,
the clan slaughtered, to see in blackness
a golden plain. Some say the cave was an altar,

the beasts sacred, but I think the task
was to get it right, the horse's leap,
the faun's terror, the lion's charge, knowing
that in a life of change those animals
would stay. They have. The ibex glowers.

Horses still snuffle the cave walls,
jaws open in surprise, eyes wide in wonder.
That's where it began, and why I slog
through rank black soil to find radiant images
with horses in high winds to guide my hand.

Love in the Afternoon

Two white butterflies
shimmy over a bed
of tulips, quivering
like a long sentence
waiting
for a main clause.
They kiss and drift apart
and kiss again,
lips open,
deeper this time.

The pair are not mating,
which they will do
back to back on a leaf,
though I cannot imagine
anything that airy
can procreate.
No, they are ballerinas
in a pas de deux
gone improvisational
and free,

moving in rhythm
with one another.
Now they quicken
like thin fingers
unbuttoning a shirt
and twining around
stiff curls
on bare skin,
until, abashed,
face flushed,

holding my breath,
I turn away

from all that radiance.
Later, they flutter
alone,
in smaller arcs,
the vowels high fliers
ungrounded
by consonants,
and sometimes
they flick my ear.

Whelk

Mud-colored outside,
sinuous, shaped
like an overgrown comma,

with gaps that reveal
a spiral inside
like the pearl brooch

my mother kept in velvet
and never wore.
I've read that the whelks

break on the journey
to shore, where they land
among perfect scallops.

I watched this one ravaged
on the road to the headland:
a gull scooped it up,

dropped it to smash the shell,
and with one hoarse shriek
touched down

to gobble its flesh.
I see the ruined shell
as I might gaze

at the headless statues
of gods and imagine
their eyes whole.

For a while
I am a maker
of whelk shells,

carving the curvy pouch,
whittling the crown,
sharpening the tail.

I hold one to my ear
and hear the settlers shout
at the smell of land

and the wreck bell ring
for drowned passengers
washed ashore.

But the shell in my hand,
split open, is mute,
a broken temple

where worshipers once stood,
keeper of what is not said,
and incomplete, as I am

shattered, in doubt,
inside chipped walls,
its silence my silence.

Green River

Grave ground can't hold them. They crowd into sight,
elbowing to show you who they were
and what they offer: sea waves in bronze
oddly near a factory plaster angel.

One gravel path connects artists and farmers,
all villagers, no other faith in common:
Jean Stafford speaks knives to Elaine de Kooning
and both lie a few graves from the Bennetts,

my locksmith's family. Frank O'Hara laughs
to see a white paint tube left as a calling card
on Jackson Pollock's boulder. I want to ask them
what the earth gave them when breath failed,

the day they tried to drip more oils,
type more words, or grind another key.
My question would dissolve in wind, the answer
obvious: all work is unfinished

by definition, in brass or on the page,
letters unread, the empty fishing net,
the riderless bike slanted against a tree
on the road to the Green River.

Cool Jazz

Late afternoon, under a salmon sky,
a night heron stalking with charcoal plumage
leaned sideways like a bowling pin off balance

on an island risen for the day
only to sink later with the tide.
I saw Miles Davis lean aslant, a night heron

on Broadway, shoulders hunched, horn pointed down,
until he hoisted brass and played away
sadness of Spain, his sadness, with a tight mute

and without vibrato, making a sound
like moaning underwater, then wider,
embracing all sound, tern cries, wind in cedars.

In the silence of a heron stabbing minnows
you could hear Miles, his hunger of another
kind, deeper, gnawing, harder to feed.

Applause rose up like water slapping the shore.
He lowered his eyes, muttered "Endings just drag me,"
and walked off the platform. The heron flew.

Tattoo

"Let your chosen object convey the feeling,"
a poet said. My student silenced earphones
blaring indie rock, and bared an arm

to show the object: a tattoo. I thought
a wingy angel or a scorpion,
or a dragonfly, such as I'd seen,

inked in lurid color to the flesh,
and wondered how it might evoke the feeling.
It was a number, 49316,

ice-blue, an upside-down triangle,
his Jewish grandmother's, five digits
branded on her arm when young, a prisoner

at Auschwitz. She survived, lived long,
and died last year. "She sat too still,
wet-kissed a lot, and never was content.

But she stroked my arm, where my tattoo is now."
Her name? "Rebecca. Rivka. She said Hashem,
her God, betrayed her." Wait, I thought, her faith

forbids body marks. My reason failed
when I remembered photographs of faces,
nameless, voiceless. Not Rivka, whose cry,

iambic, meaning *I am*, — "Survive, survive!" —
pours through her grandson, who never studied
Torah, who, in his death's-head t-shirt,

torn jeans and Reeboks, danced out to the beat
of "Hold On," jumped the stairs, two at a time,
and wrote of a wind-tossed elm. For Rivka Bloom.

FROM *The Broken String* (2007)

The Broken String

1

When Itzhak Perlman raised his violin
and felt the string snap, he sank and looked down
at legs unfit to stand and cross the stage
for a replacement. He bowed to the maestro,
played radiant chords, and finished the concerto

with the strings he had. Rage forced low notes
as this surf crashes on rock, turns and lifts.
Later, he affirmed it's what you do:
not just play the score, but make new music
with what you have, then with what you have left.

2

What you have left: Bill Evans at the keyboard,
Porgy. The sound rose, but one note, *unworthy*,
stalled in his head above the weightless chords,
above the bass, the trumpet's holler: *Porgy.*
A sudden clenched fist rose, pounded the keys,

fell limp: a heroin shot had hit a nerve.
I Loves You, Porgy. Sundays at the Vanguard
he soloed, improvised—his test that starved
nameless fear. Hands pitted against each other,
like the sea's crosscurrents, played away anger.

3

My father bowed before the Knabe piano,
scanned notes, touched fingers lightly, and began,
by some black art, I thought, his hearing gone

for years. And always, Mozart, Liszt, Beethoven.
One day I gasped, for there were runs

he never heard, played as a broken kite string
launches a lifelike eagle that might soar
on what the flier holds, what he has left.
Not even winds that howl along these shores
and raise the surf can ever ground that flight.

The Letter B

In the beginning was the letter B.
Through B, God made the world. Today that sign

gleams on a keyboard for neither cadenzas
nor waterfall arpeggios, but for prayers

tapped out on keys that flicker like strung beads,
paper-thin, like pearly yellow seashells

tide washes in. I long for weightier strokes
by surer hands with trowels that dug out sound,

B at the base. For the B that blooms now,
curved like a bellflower in high wind,

a Phoenician sailed the letter *beth*
to the Greeks for *beta*, centuries ago.

B is for B.C.E., for Nestor's cup,
for the stone scratches on a burial urn,

and for Babel's blankness when our languages
were undone; B is for bare winters

of the untaught, for slaves' songs bellowed out
on a free night, and for the blessed who learned

to write them down. B is for Hector's burial,
and for the bending of angry Achilles

who, when he remembers his own dead father
he will not see again, gives up the body,

and the Trojans buried Hector, breaker of horses.
B is for barbed rage, and for the bond

between one and another, and how the two
enfold, like buxom curves of the letter B,

and how, braided together, they brew words
benign and bellicose, brash and believing,

bits of ourselves strewn, rooted, over time.
B, the blaze of black fire on white fire,

the Torah's letters, blares at the center,
bottom row, where my lines are born.

The Fifth of July

Hot sun again. Coda to last night's flares
that rose in giant O's and fell in tears,
a lowdown blue-note soprano sax blares
"O beautiful," razz for the morning after.
Flags snap in pride, but pride flags in the fire
of headline deaths, and high convictions lie
like fizzled-out red crackers on the shore,
now litter for the pick-up volunteers.
Up headland, the tide licks ochre stones
as though to coax their spirit, one by one,
in shallows, to lift up in the clean vapor

still found in road-sign names of English settlers—
and in a photo of Moses, my great-uncle,
who grins at me now, strutting army medals
of World War I. He was prized as the first
born here to foreign parents on a past
Fourth of July. O season of sky flashes,
give me instead the lesser lights of fireflies,
milky lampshells, stars, and bayberry candles
of uncertainty, the rosebush on sand
burning but uncharred. Limitations. An old shepherd
pacing the shore at low tide, sniffing driftwood.

Query

Is there a healing twig or plume,
a rod or wizard's tea, a spell,
a paste of flowers and their stems
to lift my love and make him whole?

I'd see him take these rocky stairs
two after two, down to a park
that overflows with sycamores
whose twisted limbs have just come back

to sprout, renewed, on paths so thin,
so dense with green, he'd lose his way,
search for an iron bridge or pond,
and know, just as a ball let fly

sails back, he would walk out again.
When science shrugs, where is the stone
that mends, the dung beetle that cures.
Or, surely if some words on fire

can kill, others can right a wrong.
Shaman, teach me a chant to ban
pain. For it, take all my songs,
whose cures, if any, are unknown.

Headstones

Twin tidelines of shells gleam on wet sand
like a giant's tire tracks: fluted white chips,
cracked blues, a purple comma, shards of whelks
the Montauks whittled down to beads and strung

as wampum, shining barter for protection
against attack. What strategy, that art.
I see the Montauk sachem Wyandanch,
offered knives for land, crave only muxes—

drills for threading clamshells into necklaces.
Sell these plains, why not—only in name,
after all—besides, he would have given
land and sea, with all its whales, for peace.

Yes, he would sign their scrawled-on page, his stamp
no X but two stick figures, their hands clasped.
Hands fell as leaves. Wyandanch dead,
his language failed, names faded that had vowels

like gulls' cries: *Poniut, Sassakato,*
never on headstones. In a nameless grave,
diggers found clamshell money strung with weeds,
struck with the island's sand-and-water face,

strewn like coins in Egypt's tombs, new mintings
whose glossy hollows stored a people's prayers
and tagged the one who wore them: powerful,
now holier for being buried fire.

The town yacht club has "headstones"—gazing photos,
racing trophies. Once, as a dinner guest
I drove past roads with names of English counties,
Norfolk and Kent, then found a seaside table.

Wyandanch would not have been invited,
nor would my grandfather Dave, much less
my ancestor Schmuel, but there I was,
staring at shell toss, hearing breakers roar:

Wyandanch and *Quashashem,* his daughter,
her name the sound of seawater through stones,
snapped shells their monument, their living marker.
Sun gone, white jackets circled linen,

the voices swelled, long open vowels rolled in,
sharp consonants clicked and crackled with the surf
to drown out even the historical
cannon fire when men lowered the flag.

Blue in Green

Blue in green: baywater seen through grasses
that quiver over it, stirring the air,
slanted against the water's one-em dashes.
Each blade is a brushstroke on thin rice paper,

unrehearsed, undrafted, no revision,
right on the first take. In "Blue in Green,"
on tenor sax, John Coltrane fills the blues
with mournful chords on scales older than Jubal's,

ending in air. He'd not played it before
that recording, with that piano and bass
rising alone and, birds in flight, together.
Right on the first take. Improvisation,

he called it, but it must have been foreseen,
like the painter's brushstroke. A wrong line
could blot the composition, snag the paper.
It had to be unstudied, like a tern's cry,

and natural, like a rope's clink on a mast
with wind as bass player, huge and invisible.
If only I could remember the past
without regret for the windrose petal's fall,

for words unspoken, and without remorse
for loves withheld. Rough-draft mistakes.
If only my heart could teach my hands
to play, and get it right on the first take.

The Footbridge

Facing wisteria that turned soot-gray,
Monet painted a footbridge over a pond,
dawn, noon, sundown. Seeing neither violet

nor red, only ice blue, he gazed at willows
no longer willows, and cried for the sun
that would always outblaze new city lights.

Just as his eyesight failed, his vision grew.
In *Japanese Bridge*, green loops span two banks
as they might touch two continents. Two centuries.

Wild hair entangles someone else's dreams—
the painter's hand moved to a watery plant,
deep-set, that surfaced and broke into flame.

Here at Parson's Pond, I keep that flame.
I'd planned to cross the footbridge that goes nowhere,
with planks that snake from woods into more woods

and end in darkness. I took a safer route
instead, and saw the arch mirrored in water
where wind stirred bony legs that fell in place

intact, as though it sank and rose again.
November. No sleet as yet, no chill.
Even swamp oaks held leaves. Wind warped the pond's

mirror-footbridge into an abstraction
in fire colors, come up from silt to try me
on this clear day in my figural world.

Kol Nidrei, September 2001

All vows are canceled now,
all words undone like chains
that snap, their lockets smashed.
All sentences cut short,

main clauses powerless
to govern their dependents
or lead the voice in prayer.
All syllables annulled.

Verbs lag. All images
envisioned by blind eyes.
All penciled lines erased
that trembling hands composed.

My court, a grove at sundown:
sun rays pour through stiff branches,
unearthly yet of earth;
stump of a fallen oak

whose mate once flourished green
and now looms red and yellow
like towers burst into flame.
No ark with scrolls, no benches,

no prayer shawls, holy books,
or ram's horn. Only trees
stand witness in this silence,
and autumn's humid air

blurs a bark's crevices.
As this cloud turns to vapor,
all forms circle in smoke,
all promises unravel,

all pages torn to shreds
and blown to drift in wind
whose words cannot reveal
the truth of what I've seen.

First Nights

The best of all was listening to a hush
under the chandelier that never fell
and the fat box adorned with gilded masks.

When stiff asbestos parted over velvet,
my father gasped. He'd left the stage for a desk
when I was born. And now first nights were holy.

A program and a house called the Majestic,
more than prayer book and shul, called forth his praise.
One night an actor, fake wrinkles, white hair,

cried out under his breath, *All-shaking thunder,*
hoarse as my father, who had scared me once,
shutting a book and crying to some storm,

Arms, arms, sword, fire. That night, pitched forward,
I clutched a lineny square, but no tears came
for that desperate king until the swords

I suddenly thought real clashed for his throne.
Exits, applause, and I could breathe again.
My father said, "It helps us bear God's silences,"

and I knew watching was a kind of prayer,
a make-believe you play by looking hard.
It lifted him, as when, evenings at home,

dead still in thoughts about his sister lost,
he heard of cities bombed, while there, onstage,
Lear shouted, in a whisper, *Mad, sweet heaven.*

Thelonious Himself

They came back new each night: thumps, craggy runs,
one-finger jabs at keys that were hot pans.
Heels dug in wood, soles flapping like seals,
he stabbed notes that seemed wrong until they soared,

all ragged beauty. Just twenty-five, I envied
his starry reach, the risk to play it real.
At the slick magazine, the risk was only
no risk. I stabbed a lukewarm keyboard,

hard prose about airy tulle. Form meant neat,
no dissonance. Once I was tapped to herd
Ten Best-Dressed College Girls to hear the Monk
in a café on St. Marks Place. Not bad.

Now *there* was neatness. Strict as shorebirds grouping,
they filed in, breadknife heels clacking in tempo;
strangled waists, sleek heads acclaiming finish.
Ten S-shapes, twenty legs Monk ogled through

dark glasses, bamboo frames. He didn't sneer
at their clatter. No, while the sax wailed, solo,
Monk stood tall and swayed forward, unmistakably
davening, moved by some unseen beauty.

Suddenly he snapped fingers as though
to shape pain into order. That was form.
And all was void, as before Creation,
and there was light. I left the job next day.

Art Tatum at the Gee-Haw Stables

Hands flew across the keys like osprey wings
in high wind. Solo flight. He played alone

and cursed blurred sight, quicksilver notes unblurred.
Uptown, after hours, he cast out

the tell-it-all-to-God, blessed-be-His-name,
whatever-else-might-come fury and grief.

Uptown was where the real arpeggios soared,
in "Sweet Lorraine" and "Georgia on My Mind,"

where eyelids covered visions like an ark
as he trilled a hymn he'd picked out once

when keys danced to his father's harp, to strings
of a steel-pipe mechanic, after hours.

Here the boss tapped a whisk broom on newspaper,
and the frail stride piano outshone the grand

earlier, on Fifty-second Street,
where white faces had gasped, stunned by the speed

and accuracy of two-handed runs,
never to know that when he left there, caneless,

and taxied uptown, he, the put-on artist,
sang out after hours, and for God.

The Horror

Soutine created light
at the heart of dread
by dragging a steer's carcass
up to his rooms in Paris.

It twisted on a rack
like a tormented saint
while he watched from his easel,
casement windows shut

to shelter canvases.
When flies crowded the flesh
and hid its pinks and scarlets,
he paid a ragged model

to sit beside the corpse
and fan insects away.
Of course, it decomposed.
He hefted pails of blood

he'd carried from the market
and sloshed them over rot
to restore the gleam.
Sickened, weak from hunger

(he scarcely ate for days
to stoke a greedier fire),
Soutine attacked the canvas,
slashing with palette knife.

He slapped on reds for legs
and shoulders with a brush
that sprang in arabesques
and sucked as it pulled away

like seawater from rocks.
Fingers smeared the haunch
with white-yellow swervings
until an incandescence

leaped out of the carrion
like the sky's fire at dawn.
Garnets and rubies glowed
from the massive hulk.

He sliced air with his brush
that had transfigured it.
When neighbors reported odors
of decaying flesh,

Soutine harangued inspectors
about the health of art.
He never explained his task:
to look into death's hide

unflinching, to uncover
horror as it is,
and in a putrid room
turn flesh into light.

Death

Kaddish that sanctifies and praises being.
Black fire on moss: the grackle on the lawn
caught on fence wire, the nape still radiant,
yellow eye staring. The oak leaves I spread
that cover it. All but the yellow eye.

               ·

Loss that calls for exactitude, the urge
to render color: that bird's purple-black,
the green it fell on. The vivid thought
that changes shape and fades like a slow cloud,
scarlet azalea blossoms gone to straw.

               ·

In England's hills, a church marked by a skeleton
set over a bronze clock as though it might
gaze at daylight hours, if it had eyes;
in Mexico, on the Day of the Dead,
a girl in silk fondling her doll, a skull.

               ·

New Orleans: bystanders in undershirts,
in housedresses, follow a stranger's coffin
down to the church, to hum, croon, and ad-lib
"Call Jesus." Now the band picks up the hymn.
A sax keens low, subdued, tense with long waiting.

               ·

After the trumpet's dirge, after the burial,
jazzmen cut loose and blow the second-line beat,

up-tempo. Umbrellas open out like peonies
and spin with dancers. A snare drum seethes.
"Didn't He Ramble" raises up a life.

·

Spring rain that plays umbrellas like bass drums
soaks shoes of graveside kin who mumble Kaddish,
prayer with no word of death. Uncle Abe's sister
stands in the mire as though for penitence
and pivots from earth to fresh-cut grass.

·

The bowl she feeds him from, red-figured clay,
copied from one fired for a Spartan king
to sustain the journey. Her hand that flies
crazily off the page when she tries to sign
the DNR he ordered to let go.

·

The jewels warriors buried in Beowulf's barrow,
gold beakers and mead cups that thieves once dared
to drag from the hoard. Now let the earth have them
and cry to heaven the heirlooms are gone
that never were of use to the living.

·

Black woodsmoke that rose high over the barrow
roared to the sky and drowned their weeping
for their good lord's going. An old Geat woman
who sang grief, war, and slaughter would follow
Beowulf's time, as the sky swallowed smoke.

·

The summer day when, poised to dive from rocks
into the sea, you reached out arms that still
wrap mine in sleep. The Etruscan king and queen
on a sarcophagus, under a shroud.
Under our paisley sheet. Years of our days.

From the New World

Orange alert has glared over this city
since terror acquired colors. Orange,
not yellow, not even yellow elevated.

Before Dvořák's Ninth, at Lincoln Center,
guards worry my handbag, stuffed with war news.
Oak leaves stick to pavement, yellow-to-orange

and high orange, brightest before they wither.
This year they sadden us. Talk was of endings,
not leaves but unrecurrent lives, and yet

with others now, we sink into a hush
like sanderlings that fly on a soundless cue.
Once the composer said his symphony

was Czech, as he was, that he added
"From the New World" in the final draft,
an offering for three years in America,

but in an oboe's long, plaintive vibrato,
I hear the phrases of Hasidic melodies,
African chants, come-thou's, and kyries

I caught once on a street corner downtown,
four blocks merging like a napkin's points.
I raced a traffic light's orange-to-red

to find a synagogue confronting churches,
Baptist and Roman, eyeing one another.
High above street whines, music soared in quarrels,

moans, blues, calls-and-responses, hymns that rose up
together from stone. It took a Czech patriot
to restore that day. Now the people cheer

so loud you'd think a New World is beginning,
the clamor telling us this world will do
as long as we can have some more of it.

Outside, the fountain shoots the stars.
We glance upward, smiling, even when
a leaf spins down to concrete, crisp, high orange.

Apples

Rain hazes a street cart's green umbrella
but not its apples, heaped in paper cartons,
dry under cling film. The apple man,

who shirrs his mouth as though eating tart fruit,
exhibits four like racehorses at auction:
Blacktwig, Holland, Crimson King, Salome.

I tried one and its cold grain jolted memory:
a hill where meager apples fell so bruised
that locals wondered why we scooped them up,

my friend and I, in matching navy blazers.
One bite and I heard her laughter toll,
free as school's out, her face flushed in late sun.

I asked the apple merchant for another,
jaunty as Cezanne's still-life reds and yellows,
having more life than stillness, telling me

that, uncut, unpeeled, they are not for feasting
but for themselves, and building strength to fly
at any moment, leap from a skewed bowl,

whirl in the air, and roll off a tilted table.
Fruit-stand vendor, master of Northern Spies,
let a loose apple teach me how to spin

at random, burn in light and rave in shadows.
Bring me a Winesap like the one Eve tasted,
savored and shared, and asked for more.

No fool, she knew that beauty strikes just once,
hard, never in comfort. For that bitter fruit,
tasting of earth and song, I'd risk exile.

The air is bland here. I would forfeit mist
for hail, put on a robe of dandelions,
and run out, broken, to weep and curse — for joy.

The Row

> *A Winter Wedding, Washington Square,*
> oil on canvas, Fernand Lungren, 1897

Nothing is really lost. Take this white wedding,
for instance. After vows in the steeple church,
horse carriages file down to the Arch

along The Row, houses with Doric columns
and marble steps. A plaque or a stone lion
sets them apart, but all are the same,

and, the big snow over, one in whiteness.
Outside wrought-iron gates, men stroke silk top hats,
women wave puffed sleeves. Fashions later,

we hailed a horseless taxi near The Row,
restless before another wedding, ours,
at work until we had to leave, in jeans

to be slipped off, my dress slung on his arm.
In a house uptown, we'd stand in awe
and celebrate the mystery of marriage,

uttering *Blessed art Thou*, not in belief
but ceremony. Hadn't our bodies wed,
hadn't we whispered vows to one another,

stronger than prayers memorized and chanted?
We looked back for a sign — a tree, a sparrow,
to mark this hour. Far off, a small spark,

a match, perhaps, suddenly flamed larger,
and columns blazed. Our vows were of the present
and future, but not this past: The Row,

grand-nineties look, hints of a Greek temple,
like marriage wine, is and was, long before us.
I thought that light had gone out. I was wrong.

We pass The Row each day, and have, and will,
each of us separate, both the same,
in high sunlight or in the salmon glow

at sundown, streetlamps started, burning low.
It is always Greece, the coach-and-driver wedding,
and the cab to our own vows, all one, all now.

Late Snow

First day of spring and winter can't let go.
I can't let go, through dread, of silver maybes:
of black that glows, as a cowbird's sheen,
of gray dawns when, mud-colored, slow,

the river to the west gurgles hosannas.
Now near the end of the middle of my life,
all I want is more wakings like this one,
to watch day break, hear the trash truck growl,

glance at my love's body, shadowy
under bed linen, shaping a luminous question.
I'll have a pale sun strike the air conditioner,
turn its ice particles into asterisks,

and wake a bewitched maple that will bloom
despite the park's tossed soda cans, dope fumes,
dog piss, rat poison, banal conversation—
green as on the first day of Creation.

In Place of Belief

1

Tradition threatens. Far off, I heard bells,
those pebbly ones that top scrolls in the ark.
Up ahead, gargoyles with toothy snarls
glared from a synagogue on Central Park.

I'd read the place grew from a wooden house.
When razed, its holy innards were sent on
to other temples: lamps, goblets for wine,
pointers, and floorboards that soak up prayers.

Once, turning thirteen, called to the ark,
I touched a scroll whose black letters blurred
like scuff marks on sand the sea had washed.
I listened for God's bass and heard instead

chatter, a squeaky platform. Shuddering,
how could I even mumble sacred songs.
Only now, through doors of a massive building
whose ark is curtained shut, silver bells ring.

2

Lao Tsu told it best: The way is nameless.
The real cannot be seen. Still I make lists
of miracles, and never mind eternal.
Here, lilies unfurl in rocky soil;

a papery plant blooms into silver dollars;
grackles bob in a ring like a holy synod.
Earthly, but so was God's roll call of items
to build a chest for the Law: acacia wood,

brass rings, indigo curtains, names of things
transient but fit to hold all that endures.
Whatever comes, the voice that follows lightning
or Billie's tones, the hush after she sings;

the cloud that inks the field or my neighbor's shadow,
liquid in moonlight, I would eavesdrop, spy,
and keep watch on the chance, however slight,
that the unseen might dazzle into sight.

3

An image reveals what we're afraid we mean.
In Nadar's print, a banker's palm lies empty,
rigid as a saint's in benediction,
and coppery, as though it still holds money.

Of course. An actor tells me it is gesture,
not utterance, that contradicts a line,
the twisted silk scarf a dead giveaway,
the woman's knife marks on the table linen,

more than clipped words, disclose her wrath.
You turn from ritual, though once you stood solemn
at our unorthodox wedding, in the faith
but bare of symbols, and suddenly fished satin

from a side pocket to cover your head.
For your father, you explained. I nodded,
and said no more. Such lapses have been rare
in you, loyal to science and human care.

4

Hands are truth-tellers, sometimes informers,
and treacherous. They creep out of disguises.

The gilt hand a friend gave me in Cancun,
blessed by a priest, points to the work undone.

Rodin carved hands that beg, clench, rise in anger,
or throb in sex, revealing the invisible
bodies they serve. One pair of hands in marble
shapes a cathedral's tower, with tapered fingers

that touch as a clamshell shuts — in love, in fear.
Henri Matisse lived as an unbeliever
but for one hand that sketched hands locked in prayer.
And you, like Flaubert's Dr. Larivière,

practice virtue without believing in it.
Now you reach for a twig to stake clematis
with hands always ungloved to palpate flesh
and probe a virus strain that causes death.

5

Autumn, and Hopkins first glimpsed silver-on-silver
Northern Lights, which roused "delightful fear"
as rays pulsed like a sun bursting through clouds.
Notes wrestle in his journals; side by side

some challenge God, others caress the whorls
he called star knots in a thick, weathered aspen,
yew leaves, the horned violet, the bluebell,
the ruck and crease of waves that flash through stones.

I thought of Hopkins and his praise today
when I studied the pure symmetry
of cross-stitches on an oak leaf's underside,
and knew that love is nothing less than accuracy:

the fire that I lit this morning flares
sapphire and violet as it gasps for air;

the blackening logs, the smell of cedar wood
are what I have of an evasive God.

6
      To Hedda Sterne

The painter spoke at last: "My dark is luminous.
For those who see, the sun's glare can obscure
sharp outlines." When she wheeled her chair toward mine,
blank eyes questioned the dahlias I gave her.

Walls are stripped of canvases, the ladder gone
that she had climbed to paint angles of light,
where brushstrokes had flown in constant motion
but with no fixed point, like her faith and art.

Suddenly she waved my hand aside
and, trembling, but with startling exactness,
poured sherry for us both in crystal glasses.
"Shapes are vague now, but I have memorized

the clock, the *OED*, the china shelf."
She pointed to them — in the wrong locations.
Art does not ask fidelity to life
but ardent precision. So does belief.

Readers

> *St. Anne Teaching the Virgin to Read,*
> *Juan de Juni, Valladolid Cathedral, Spain*

It's the persimmon in St. Anne's hand
as she teaches the Virgin to read,

the parchment, grainy, cool as leaves, the binding,
the sly glance, the bodies coarse and dense,

as mother and daughter, carved in radiant wood,
search for words. Hands are not joined,

but what is that compared with eyes that burn,
red-yellow gowns that fall to the floor as one.

The child touches letters M and MA
for Mary, like the Chinese brushstroke moon,

Hebrew *mem*, Greek *mu*, the Babylonian
mas mas mas of the student who digs signs

in earth and notches clay. Shaped like a bridge,
suspended, the raised M links two cultures,

two readers. It's touch that stirs words off pages,
even for the monk who inked a bible,

drew saints' heads in the crooks of L's,
then ran his fingers lightly down the jewels

on gold covers. And it is the hunger,
as in this Mary's eyes, to know the letters

that peer through letters, to find the writer
before the writer, and for all the mysteries

of the flesh, the fruit, the word, the story:
Persimmon. Parchment. Try it: *Mama, Mary*.

Chosen

My own possessions books and one great love,
I marvel at how Leonardo's Virgin
looks up from words to hear the one Word: *chosen*.

Now here's a saltier miracle of birth:
No Gabriel, but St. John of the waters
has blessed a sign, TERNS NESTING, in streaked letters,

stuck on a sandy lane fenced with thin wire
to make a wall you feel but do not see.
Read FOOTPATH, and enter at your peril.

Not song but shrieks. Wingflaps. White birds dip fast
and wheel, a black-capped sky patrol, their eggs
the colors of rock and pied for camouflage.

The chicks hatched—odor of moss, slime, algae—
red bills struck out to sea, they drop for fish
one by one by one, sliding down air.

Don't glance at their young. And don't lose heart
or sink in quicksand while envying quick flight.
Onshore, walkers are weighty, each alone,

faint smiles, eyes low, and only footprints cross.
Random, directionless. Not so these fliers.
They're picked to breed *ternness*, chosen for

the hunter's scan, the dive, the climb. And I,
whose heirs are words, wish for them: fly,
terns, ride long over water and survive.

Walk!

> *Arise, and take up thy bed, and walk.*
> —Mark 2:9

Rise up and stagger now on the sea road
at sunset, where clouds vanish like bandages

that fall from cured flesh, where lavender nods.
Wade through wild roses poking up through sand.

At low tide, a green island looms so close
that, though fumbling, you might trudge through water,

never mind leap or glide, and reach dry sand.
Once you strode high, unbending, and you fell

like a tree. When strangers helped you rise,
a smile masked rage. Science your guide, you'd been

the healer, not the healed. Days of rain
when others shot the stairs, leaped into waves,

swam inlets. Bend to the knife. And even after,
you said, no miracle. A surgeon's skill.

But here are wonders. You limp past scrub pines
and hear the salt wind play a lyre-shaped oak.

Wake to flaws; the sea tosses back shells
brightest when they are chipped, snapped, and broken.

Queen Hermione, perfect in stone,
stirs, steps off a fluted post, and stumbles,

never to soar. We slog. We tramp the road
of possibility. Give me your arm.

Harp Song

Near the shore, this white oak split in two
struggles to endure sea winds and grow,
twin columns chapped and branches stripped of leaves.

The bark is grooved like an islander's face
as he sails out for bass with pots and trawl,
and in the worst storms sings in a raspy,

whiskey voice haul-aways learned from whalers.
While gale-force winds snapped the unbending hickory,
lashed a cedar, and ripped out an elm

in acid soil worn smooth and unsustaining
even of grass, the doubled oak goes on.
Both arms reach skyward. The trunk is bent

into a U, the shape of a harp, unstrung.
In gales, it slides from one note to another,
portamento, like a soprano's glide.

I breathe deep when I pass: a song of rage
rises from wood that has been salt-bleached, cut,
whipped to buckle, and instead, stands fast.

Tempests roll out chords, pick the harp-tree clean
with pizzicati, and weave eerie arpeggios.
I have heard wooden harps whose strings fell slack

for centuries—one cast down when Deor,
once a king's prized singer of battle songs,
found a new harpist in his chair at court,

his own name lost, and moaned: *it, too, may pass*;
but this harp cries out *survive* in anger,
stringless, played by winds, to a silent god.

Waves

The burst, the lilt and rock, the wheel of spray,
the flash of waves exploding in hard rain.

Perhaps they are the dead, their watermark
the signatures of shipwrecked passengers,

or coded messages from men and women
desperate to tell what they have seen.

Speed, thunder, surprise. The jarring thump
of low bass drums, the dancer's leap and bow,

the gospel singer's growl, the pause, the shout,
dodging the beat, notes jammed with syllables,

the hums, mumbles, and cries, the choruses,
cymbals that gleam in sudden white-gold light.

Breakers roared when Caedmon sang Creation
in a new verse with the rhythmic pull of oars.

Rollers boom on a shore I cannot see
and tie me to flood-dead, quake-dead, war-dead,

disaster-dead, or dead ripped from the stars.
As I trudge in the shallows, sliding in wrack,

order snapped apart like a broken string,
each end still aloft, trembling in air,

the sea ahead, the roadways drowned behind,
a wave shimmers, taking its time to fall.

How all that matters is to stand fast
on the ridge that's left, and hear the music.

FROM *Days of Wonder* (2003)

Repentance of an Art Critic, 1925

"Existe-t-il une peinture juive?"
—Fritz Vanderpyl

Some learned the palette is the devil's platter,
the brush a crucifix: by law, no icons,
no graven images "made unto thee."

Yet Soutine dries creeds in the Paris sun,
his strokes prayers for pardon. Others are freer.
A mystery. I find no common style,

no *ism,* nest for thought, as in a pen stand.
Marc Chagall's villages, Soutine's dead turkeys,
Sonia Delauney's rings, make an odd stew.

In Kisling's painting, Kiki of Montparnasse
lies on flowered silk. Nearby, a window opens
on more windows. Air, light. Still I say,

could Michelangelo have carved *La Pietà*
without belief, his trust only in stone?
Even Rouault, godless, hunted by God,

painted Christ's head slashed with lines. How faith crushes
and builds. But not them. Torn up from dry soil,
replanted, pruned back, they blossom again

like horse chestnuts under a new god.
Their only faith, if one can call it that,
lurks in this day's sunlit buildings, leaves

that still sparkle with raindrops, and brushstrokes
that catch the glimmer. Some fled pogroms.
But take Modigliani, from Livorno,

whose women, swans, gaze with clouded pupils.
The painter's stare. Doorlocks pried open,
they blink under puff-clouded skies,

talk at Le Dôme until the paint runs free,
then, each to his easel, gather beliefs
like lilies that die as the canvas blooms.

Can the most foreign of the new Parisians
share anything besides a lost law?
I've said no. Was I wrong? I ask Kisling,

who waves at his painting. It seizes me,
and a voice rises from so deep I know
it cannot be my own: the sheer exactness

of bowl, knife, apple, keeps us from loss
by capturing the day that does not end.
In Kisling's vision of his studio,

two forms stand at either end of a table:
within the oil is his oil of a nude
darting furtive glances, and Modigliani's

long head. Between them are paintbrushes
poised like rockets waiting to explode,
a pipe, a half-filled glass, and a hand of cards.

Flags

Red, yellow banners on sloops in the bay
catch the erratic wind; each with one pattern,
distinct, indelible, soars like a phrase
heard once that resounds over the waves' din.

My father stood without a flag in silence,
an advertising man, stunned when his client,
a mill owner, routinely called the carders
of color, or of foreign birth, "those others."

Once, called to the silver-and-gilt table
where custom had a dinner guest say grace,
his turn came. With crushed rage he knew
he'd passed, "A" for "Accepted." Speech came slow

when he tried to say, "You will drown in lies."
Instead, he lifted a white handkerchief,
knotted the corners, clapped it to his head,
and chanted, *Baruch atah adonai* . . .

to a startled host. Now I hear his prayer
that's printed in bold letters on a handkerchief
among red, yellow flags beyond the wharf,
as I grope for words in the mist-thick air.

The Last Meeting

Danzig, 1932

All I have of the last visit to Germany,
my father keen to show his New World bride,
is this photo: a sleek lad and his father
are sentinels; each man clutches a chair,

arms flexed to hold up beams of a falling house.
My mother bends to curb lank arms and legs
that trail generations of New York and Kansas.
Dad's mother has a farmer's mottled hands,

skin pleated by the sun. With set jaw, wordless,
she had begged them to stay; there would be peace.
The photo is stamped "Danzig," city of change:
now Germany, now Poland, now between,

and that year what Dad called "safe on first."
To Warsaw, his past, he dared not return.
My mother is younger than I am now.
She was always young. In Berlin, she had guessed

people wore armbands with Vedic signs
to show that they were blind. In this split second,
long fingers stroke her mother-in-law's shoulder
as if to skim a lake. My mother stares

with her elder's eyes at the camera lens.
Dad's sisters, home from college, glance away.
One would be shot to death, another beaten.
But my mother is Ruth in a knitted suit,

who vows to a farmhand in a peasant blouse:
Whither thou goest I will go. Where thou diest . . .
Now on my lawn I cry: Don't stay in Germany!
Come back on the last ship. Let me be born.

Jewish Cemetery, Eleventh Street

This is no place for death. No rangy weeds,
no leafy trees. No long drive to a meadow.
There's nothing like an urban cemetery,
stuck between buildings, students loping by,

to teach us all the measure of our days.
Today a walker whistles by the graveyard.
A shopper leans a bag against the gate
and hunts names through black spikes: one, *ISAAC HARBY*,

d. 1838, is blurred on stone.
I looked him up. He was a translator
of Hebrew prayers many would save unaltered.
Biographies that tell all reveal nothing,

but I know Harby dug for English words
like quartz to cut and polish until they glistened.
Dying, he read the psalms out loud to friends.
I think the line that came with his last breath

must have been *For thou, Lord, hast made me glad*,
words that danced on. A spectral Isaac Harby
who caught art-talk next door, site of the Grapevine,
now leaps to current titles at the cinema

and blesses the tomb-seer in agate phrases.
I bend to scoop up pebbles for his grave
and rattle the locked gate. When I walk on,
faces beam out at me, restless as verbs.

Job's Question on Nevis

"Turn back!" was all she snapped out as she passed
in a red dress that caught sunrays through mist.
I saw her lurch upwind, kick off spiked heels,
climb out to the edge of a knife-sharp rockpile,

and, arms outstretched, lead the sea's tympani,
lure the din, guiding the steamy waves
to shore. *Will the Almighty answer me?*
she sang out to the ocean's rising octaves,

as blown palms pointed scarflike fronds to land.
Earlier that Sunday, she had prayed
to a black Christ in a church on the island,
droned verses for a safe calm, and trekked homeward

to board white louvered windows for the storm.
She had refused the chapel's sanctuary
to ask the ocean why the wind ripped homes
and would again. Her anger captured me,

and stayed when I saw rain glaze red ginger,
drench trumpets islanders call yellow-bells,
and soak ixora. Bonelike bits of shells
and conchs lay on the beach as on an altar.

Silent, I watched her. Under a blank sky,
where waves broke over coral, in thick haze,
pitched forward to hear the whirlwind's reply,
she shook a fist, then opened hands in praise.

Grandmother's Sea

roars in my closet, oil on wood, gilt frame.
"This was your birthplace. Yes, Bensonhurst, Brooklyn.

Before subways, the ocean hissed on sand
and bluefish leaped at sunrise." Her deep voice

gathered force like sea waves. Outside the window,
a gas-tank truck rattled down her syllables

and groaned at a neighbor's door. In the painting
a woman stood, wind-tousled, with a basket

of plums on a brief panhandle of shore,
gazing at water. Except for her blue apron,

brushstrokes were murky—auburn dress, mud sky.
My grandmother wore white embroidered shirtwaists

when she stirred iron pots and tended roses.
One day I dabbed the painting with a cloth.

Dust gone, the drab seawater shone cerulean.
On shore an egret was a blazing question,

its yellow bill a penpoint under skies
of prophetic light. A tern hovered so close

to cliffs so sharp that fish stench filled the air.
Under backing, words loomed, scratched on wood:

"Ellen Terry starring in *The Good Hope*."
Artist's name blurred. Not Brooklyn. Still I know

that even after subways came, the sea
rasped outside the garden of my first house.

Steps

"And down and down and down,"
the toddler's mother sings
as he clears every ledge.

Midway we cross their path.
In rain, the museum's steps
loom like the Giant's Stairway

to Guardi's Ducal Palace.
"And up and up and up"
is what I do not say

as you stagger for balance.
Once I'd scaled that summit,
hunted over the crowd,

and saw you below, holding
two hot dogs and white roses;
you vaulted, took the steps

two at a time, then three,
and leaped to where we met.
Your smile is broader now.

You see more. On this day
of wavering, we hear
a Triton blow the horn

where Giotto's Magi open
hands that rise in air:
up, and up, and up.

FROM *The Paintings of Our Lives* (2001)

Prayer

For Agha Shahid Ali

Yom Kippur: wearing a bride's dress bought in Jerusalem,
I peer through swamp reeds, my thought in Jerusalem.

Velvet on grass. Odd, but I learned young to keep this day
just as I can, if not as I ought, in Jerusalem.

Like sleep or love, prayer may surprise the woman
who laughs by a stream, or the child distraught in Jerusalem.

My Arab dress has blue-green-yellow threads
the shades of mosaics hand-wrought in Jerusalem

that both peoples prize, like the blue-yellow Dome of the Rock,
like strung beads-and-cloves, said to ward off the drought in Jerusalem.

Both savor things that grow wild—coreopsis in April,
the rose that buds late, like an afterthought, in Jerusalem.

While car bombs flared, an Arab poet translated
Hebrew verses whose flame caught in Jerusalem.

And you, Shahid, sail Judah Halevi's sea as I,
on Ghalib's, course like an Argonaut in Jerusalem.

Stone lions pace the sultan's gate while almonds bloom
into images, Hebrew and Arabic, wrought in Jerusalem.

No words, no metaphors, for knives that gore flesh
on streets where the people have fought in Jerusalem.

As this spider weaves a web in silence,
may Hebrew and Arabic be woven taut in Jerusalem.

Here at the bay, I see my face in the shallows
and plumb for the true self our Abraham sought in Jerusalem.

Open the gates to rainbow-colored words
of outlanders, their sounds untaught in Jerusalem.

My name is Grace, Chana in Hebrew—and in Arabic.
May its meaning, "God's love," at last be taught in Jerusalem.

God Speaks

Before the hour I cried, "Let there be light!"
I tossed out some three hundred early versions.
Revisions help. What clatter in the firmament,
though, when mountains fell, stars fizzled out.

This work is my best, at least for now.
I called. I named each thing, and "it was so."
I cannot tell you how, from heaven to seas
to people, all sprang up wanting to be.

The methods I advise are more precise—
Noah's ark, for instance, gopher wood,
three stories high, side entrance, and a window.
Here when I said "the waters," oceans rose.

Worlds are never finished, only abandoned.
Yet this one came alive when there were woods
for creeping things, dry land for men and women,
the evening and the morning. *They* were good.

Creation had been done before, of course—
in legend. Same formless waste and darkness,
but with one change: the Babylonians
have many gods. Always I work alone.

Eve's Unnaming

Not horses, but roan
against the blue-green bay,

not crocuses, but wings
folded over suns,

not rhododendrons, but fire that wilts
to straw in the rain.

How to tag
stone, shell, gull,

hands enfolding lamb's-ear,
a bee sucking the delphinium,

when the sea writes and revises,
breaks, pours out, recoils,

when the elm's leaves
turn silver at dawn.

To see in the dark
the south window strew flowers

on the chapel floor,
or wind peel a sand rose,

is unnamable,
like joy,

like my love's grin
between a cap and a jacket.

Names are for things
we cannot own.

Chaim Soutine

Hunger was bearable, but not their voices
resonant as clock chimes in his head:
Thou shalt not make unto thee any graven image.

Gaunt, bleary-eyed, he filched coins from a shelf,
not for food, but for red and yellow pencils
to draw a madman who had God's fixed stare.

Locked in a cellar, grasping at cracks of light,
unrepentant, he heard his parents wail,
Or any likeness of anything in heaven above;

he sketched the rabbi, trying to uncover
red-yellow rays beneath the prayer shawl.
Thrashed, he left his village of Smilovitch

and painted. Years passed. Over and again
he'd make a still life of a dead goose, hen —
or that is in the earth beneath —

this one a hanging turkey, beak agape,
wings splayed as though still flying. Days and nights
he jabbed red-yellow strokes on canvas

to make the wingspread, damning, pitying
wings that reach for light and, falling, rise —
or that is in the water under the earth —

burned wings of Icarus; his father's hands,
gnarled fingers mending coats, the hands of Christ.
Where God had been, the turkey shone, flesh-colored

as naked man, over "Soutine," in blood,
and he sang to drown their sobbing, now grown louder:
Thou shalt not make unto thee any graven image.

Poem Ending with a Phrase from the Psalms

Here where loss spins the hickory's dry leaves,
rolls miles under wheels, and bleaches reeds
that shone wine-red, I invoke a rose
still rising like a choir, past its prime
on a spindly bush that bore scarce blooms,
as I wake to hear a jay screech like a gate
swung open, and see your hand enfolding mine
on linen: *teach us to number our days.*

Psalm for an Anniversary

Praise to boredom: to the summer solstice,
to our long marriage, its minutes dissolving
into hours here on the roof at sunset
as we watch shadows print their towers on buildings

while impersonal windows blink and darken.
Praise to recurrences: worn benches, laughter,
white roses you brought home, old army talk
I want to hear again. Bless the ruptures

healed, faint as wire dolls in the park below us—
the skiff I boarded once that coursed the bay,
leaving your island; that was urgency,
not this, when voices fall, eased by the sky's

arc over a bridge. In lulls, the mind
can see another city above this one,
ironic, hybrid as a string of puns.
Cupolas and the pyramids cut the skyline;

a red-brick campanile shelters a water tank;
and nuns in their high habits sail in pairs
to a ruined chapel over a warehouse,
its empty sockets glaring salmon pink.

A frieze of horses has survived—that is,
in replica—as though it were eternal,
while we, flawed with mistakes, who thought the skins
we shed would be our last, survey a steeple,

a tower clock, a dome. Praise to the sun
that flares and flares again in fierce explosions
even after sunset, to muddy rivers
that glow vermilion now, to second chances.

No Strings

> *Marble seated harp player, Cycladic,*
> *early third millennium B.C.*

At times your silences call back a harpist
that glows, pale yellow marble in late sun,
carved in the Cyclades, maker unknown,

seated, the head thrown back, arms gliding free,
hands curved to pluck a harp shaped like an alpha,
stringless, frame joined to shoulder, branch to tree.

The time: nearly five thousand years ago.
One hour ago. As when we met, a lifetime,
a minute past. We gazed at it, at him,

that day and the bare harp rang, drowning out
the museum's clamor and a traffic siren.
How song flows out of awe that grows in silence,

and how all things begin, alpha, with song.
At last you said the statue came along
when someone, name obscure, offered a prayer,

plied emery, and buffed a man on a chair
who'd raise a stringless harp and play the air.
Nodding, I thought of seeing in the wings

of a hushed hall a flutist who looked up
while fingering imaginary stops,
then strode onstage and made cadenzas soar.

Blue Dawn

I see Viola float in on a plank
from the wreck, touch land, pocket a seashell
for luck, and, shivering, glide into a kingdom,

as once Long Island's settlers trudged ashore
and, though weary, took in blue-green forests
at sunrise, before lines furrowed the oak trees.

When his ship steamed into New York Harbor,
my father stood on deck in cramped, thin shoes
and watched blue rocks grow to be Ellis Island.

Sailing through fog at daybreak, his eyes burning
with the statue's unlit torch, how could he know
that one day he would walk on asphalt pavement

wearing a tweed coat, though still in cramped shoes.
Scant time for shops, he said, but I knew he chose
to save the blue wonder of what might be,

as I do now: slate flagstones going blue
in the not-yet-risen sun, an unopened iris,
the miracle of a yet unprinted page.

American Solitude

The cure for loneliness is solitude.
— Marianne Moore

Hopper never painted this, but here
on a snaky path his vision lingers:

three white tombs, robots with glassed-in faces
and meters for eyes, grim mouths, flat noses,

lean forward on a platform, like strangers
with identical frowns scanning a blur,

far off, that might be their train.
Gas tanks broken for decades face Parson's

smithy, planked shut now. Both relics must stay.
The pumps have roots in gas pools, and the smithy

stores memories of hammers forging scythes
to cut spartina grass for dry salt hay.

The tanks have the remove of local clammers
who sink buckets and stand, never in pairs,

but one and one and one, blank-eyed, alone,
more serene than lonely. Today a woman

rakes in the shallows, then bends to receive
last rays in shimmering water, her long shadow

knifing the bay. She slides into her truck
to watch the sky flame over sand flats, a hawk's

wind arabesque, an island risen, brown
Atlantis, at low tide; she probes the shoreline

and beyond grassy dunes for where the land
might slope off into night. Hers is no common

emptiness, but a vaster silence filled
with terns' cries, an abundant solitude.

Nearby, the three dry gas pumps, worn
survivors of clam-digging generations,

are luminous, and have an exile's grandeur
that says: In perfect solitude, there's fire.

One day I approached the vessels
and wanted to drive on, the road ablaze

with dogwood in full bloom, but the contraptions
outdazzled the road's white, even outshone

a bleached shirt flapping alone
on a laundry line, arms pointed down.

High noon. Three urns, ironic in their outcast
dignity—as though, like some pine chests,

they might be prized in disuse—cast rays,
spun leaf-covered numbers, clanked, then wheezed

and stopped again. Shadows cut the road
before I drove off into the dark woods.

Young Woman Drawing, 1801

> *Attribution changed from Jacques-Louis David to Constance*
> *Charpentier, and later, to Marie-Denise Villers, 1774–1821*

Subject and maker shed their names, and here
the Met displays that multinominal picture
on a brochure: self-portrait of the artist,
perhaps, ageless. She is not setting out,

pale in an empire dress, nor packing shawls
in a carriage trunk. As she sits forward, still,
she hopes only to gaze into a mirror
in shadow, sunlight falling on blank paper,

until her penstrokes dance, and ever after,
to slough off names and be one-who-has-seen-
glass-shine. How did it bloom in her, this hidden
boldness? Peering out from under wisps of amber

hair strayed from a chignon, taking pencil
to outsize sketchpad, she keeps a dark vigil,
while behind her, outside a shattered pane,
proud lovers laugh on a terrace in bright sun.

Margaret Fuller

The sea churns up a ghost of the *Elizabeth*,
sunk here in 1850, with the woman
who thought herself half man when she learned Latin
early in Cambridge, who honed a keen wit

"to keep the heart from breaking." All in all,
land sighted, others rescued, lulls in the gale,
I'd say she could have swum to shore. She had
that way with danger. In Scotland once,

trapped on a ledge, she danced cold mist away.
In Rome, she nursed the wounded, wrote of war,
but could not press her thoughts into one form
"for all the tides of life that flow within me."

How to return, when long ago she knew
everyone worth knowing here, when she
who shot the rapids stuck in Boston's craw.
And how to tell them of her love, Ossoli,

and of their new republic, lost — the rebels
dead, Rome gone. Twelve hours she had that morning
to swim homeward after the brig struck shoal.
Perhaps she stalled on the foredeck, avoiding

a half-welcoming shore; perhaps she spun
through waves, then turned, as a bird veers in flight
to glimpse its mate, and saw her lover caught
with their son, half native, half Italian,

watched breakers wrench the mainmast from the hull,
cried out once, twice, into the lashing wind,
then lost her torn self to the sea's wholeness.
Once in a storm, I found washed up on sand

a jetty's pole, and saw in it my own
splintered life's course. Before that gale,
I had swum partway out to her, and sea-miles
rolled out like the decades since she drowned.

Now I stand fast. Fire Island's opal
bay at high tide sucks amber rocks shot through
with quartz-glass silica, once El Dorado
to settlers half Old World and half New.

Far off, the lighthouse shines occulting beams
on sunken draggers. Only the sea is whole.
A split log or a chipped but vacant shell
the hermit crab crawls under is my home.

The Dancers

Turning to leave, she stands before a mirror
that picks up lights in sherry-colored hair.
A black/white picture's tucked inside the frame:
she and my father stand before that same

silvery mirror hung in her parents' house
in Brooklyn. He wears a tuxedo. She's
tossed a kimono over a satin dress,
hair brushed back and cropped like Sylvia Sidney's.

They're caught winging the air, kicking a high
rag as on a tightrope, showing off glossy
smiles to Uncle Josh, who tilts the camera—
before he spins and winds up the Victrola

to play "Blue Skies." Song ended, they will gather
swimsuits for after-revels near the shore,
and a beaded purse, then step off into stars.
It's the Depression. Dad is an actor

out of work. No money, no despair.
How could they know that I'd be born to shouts
of war; his family lost. Why do I fear
now for those bright kids dancing on the night

they went to a party in the sputtering Ford,
the job with rumble seat and running boards,
the mirror behind them catching the glimmer
of my father's top hat, my mother's hair.

Brooklyn Bridge

From the beginning, it was life or death,
the maker and his son lost to the river
their bridge would hold down — one struck by a ferry,

the other by caisson bends — young Roebling's wife
learning math to redeem the family prophecy:
"It will be beautiful." And so it was, and is,

corseted to brace not merely horsecars
but trucks. Now, the sky vast after dense buildings,
I wander under Gothic towers and watch

trapezoids spring skyward, spun wire ropes
quivering in sunlight. All around me
today, like dancers stepping with unknown partners,

men and women travel east to Brooklyn,
set-jawed, some with kids in strollers,
then meet and sidle past those striding west.

"Cyclists dismount!" an unseen caller shouts,
and bikers obey. The crowd breaks for a woman
who lugs a canvas. Buckling some, she tacks

into the wind, not letting go. A man
carries roses, blooms pointed down. Some wild hope
in their striding cries "It will be beautiful,"

and raises ghosts: where walkway meets the road,
a vision of my grandmother in 1920,
belled skirt, braided red hair. She slithers under

her stalled Ford and out again, tarred black,
then cranks the engine. The cargo, prints
she's engraved on woodblocks with penlike

gouges kept on shelves, riling my grandfather
until he uttered "Flora!" twice, and cursed
the inky floors, then tromped out, slammed the door.

At twelve she'd walked the bridge to mark shirt collars
in a factory. Married young, she longed
to make black collars; she saw waves and sea

reversed to hazard what would be when wood
was pressed to paper, dreams caught in intaglio.
She drove from Brooklyn through cathedral windows,

past rude stares, to show her prints in "the city,"
smoothing a crumpled New York driver's license,
one of the first earned by a woman, and bearing

four invisible words: "It will be beautiful."
She built no bridge, but crossed this steel
and sand-colored granite arched over schooners

that killed before it joined, that said it's not
just striving, but the risk. With the fixed gaze
of one drawn to hard tasks, she finds me, frowns,

slides into the Ford, and rattles on.
Now, seeing caissons planted in the riverbed,
firm as punctuation, I trek the arch

in wonder. On the Manhattan turnoff,
a road sign reads BRIDGE, white arrow pointing left.
Once you're in that lane, you can't turn back.

Elegy Written in the Conservatory Garden

In memory of Irving Howe

Hearing the news, we headed for this garden,
a children's picture-book, a black-and-white
movie turned to color for the Oz scenes.

We'd planned to bring him here. In an arbor,
crabapple trees enclose us like a vault,
their branches splayed like nerve-ends over us.

It is before the soul has slipped from the body.
He is the blurred form moving through warped trees
like fingers on a harp. I say at last,

"In summer, when we walked in the meadow
he swore the lilacs spurred him more than quarrels."
(Later, I read he'd whispered to a friend,

"In Paris once, alone on a stone bench
between rose shrubs, I knew
that death, if it meant coming into that,

might be all right.") I say, "And even now
I know he's here, behind a screen of roses,
fragrant, pink-to-golden in the sun—

but not the man we knew, who argued hotly
about a film until the café closed."
You listen, frown, and look past the green edge

where towers poke out of elms the park's designers
hoped would hide the city's pipes, and squint
at the hospital where you tend the sick

and where you left him alive hours ago.
You don't know why he died so suddenly.
For you, true faith is evidence. I watch

your hands sort twigs to brace a fallen aster:
they are splinting a child's arm.
I say, "This garden may be paradise—"

and hesitate. It is too soiled for heaven,
too various: nasturtiums shine, their odor
of cocoa mulch merges with hints of urine;

a sea-blue bottle lies smashed on the walk;
boys in grimy shirts sketch daffodils.
On asphalt, blossoms mix with candy wrappers

or cling to grooves, white yellowing like newsprint.
Look: by our feet, a toddler rips out a rose.
We do not stop her. It is her angel.

We haven't said his name. A handbill tells us
crocuses and lilies store food underground—
perhaps where we have stored his rimless glasses.

Now, flicking a petal from your shoulder,
you say, "We'll see the spirea last through summer
and watch it turn all golden in the autumn."

I shudder at the word *autumn*.
I've read that ancient cycads grew with dinosaurs
and stood with Adam in the Garden of Eden.

We stand, as though to visit him again,
and touch a magnolia tree that may live forever,
with our thumbprints gleaming on its trunk.

Henry James Revisiting, 1904

Streets "bristle" for me, as when you returned
to lash skyscrapers and cheer the low skylines
of Washington Square. Your bare tribute, "noble,"

to La Farge's painting in Ascension Church,
makes me surmise you were wordless in wonder
at how that tiny chapel could contain

the altarpiece with an American
largeness: lank disciples watch the god soar
until seeing is all they are. You are.

I am. And now I see you struck, then stricken
as you scrawl "doom" in fear of towers to come.
I write to tell you that Ascension stands.

Angels in rows like reeds still sing the flight
high in a brownstone gifted with American
clarity: sun filters through glass saints,

strews roses on the nave, and tells of light
forever, as from fields, not cramped back yards.
It's an American slant on survival.

Tall buildings crowd row houses, not Ascension,
a landmark, *l* for long life. White pear blossoms
fall. Ascension rises. Some things remain:

ailanthus trees that smell of constant summer,
and this church spire, ascended till it's turned,
things being what they are in town, immortal.

The Designer's Notebook

E. McKnight Kauffer, 1890–1954

After you died, I opened it. *Design
is order . . . Triangle, fire; circle, water;
cube, earth. Signs of order.* How trim you were
in paisley tie, wool suit, jacquard scarf flung

over wide shoulders. Even at work,
crisp shirt, sleeves rolled to one inch of the elbow.
Silver-voiced, exact, you snapped out geometric
angles for sun on water. And your studio

held soldierly rows of sharp new pencils,
brushes fanned out in jars like peacock's tails.
Your painting, *Flight*, hid a cracked wall:
throaty honks and wing-flaps in a squall

ordered by form; white-black birds rise above
the earth in trapezoids, wingspreads of planes.
Your fires raged unseen, wild birds restrained
by the shapes you caught them in. They will live

flawlessly, as you did — seemed to, really.
The perfect shell you gave me, and the spiral
caught in a crystal globe, recall the symmetry
scratched out in tetrahedrons at your table.

What did those shapes conceal? Street crowds below
rushed under your posters. You wrote: *People
standing on corners, leaning out of windows,
swarming: young, old; arms, legs; bodies in hell.*

Words crossed out. *Raids in Europe, though as yet
here only grit whirls in air.* Turn the page:
"God have mercy upon us" someone cut
on wood—a poster—in the London plague.

Design orders. Your daughter left behind
in England. War. Forced flight. And, near the end,
when you were painting faceless, eyeless heads—
charcoal, of Edgar Allan Poe—in dread

of time passing, you scrawled five words:
Poe's fear of insanity. Inherited.
I shuddered, and I knew I'd have to look
at them one day. Back then I shut the book.

The Paintings of Our Lives

The Annunciation Triptych,
Robert Campin, the Cloisters

I

Through leaded windowpanes, the light pours down
less on the holy figures than on objects
waiting to be used, that tell the story:
a fringed towel hung askew, a kettle-laver,

unlit wall sconces, the windblown pages
of a book laid open on a table,
an empty bench the Virgin leans against
as she sits on the floor reading the bible,

not even noticing the angel Gabriel.
Those things, enlarged, furnish the Campin Room,
set here as though a great wave had spewed out
details grown to life-size replicas —

the window, firescreen, candles, gleaming kettle,
an untenanted bench roped off in velvet.
Gathered to fit a corner or a shelf,
those imitations lack the painter's order,

his art of reconciling all that varies:
the red of the Virgin's gown, repeated
in a guard's doublet and in Joseph's tunic,
binds one who sees and one who turns away.

2

Somewhere are the paintings of our lives,
invisible to us — hers, for example,
as she sits fixed on Proust, not looking up.
Across the room, a concert grand piano

once played every day stands quiet now.
It dwarfs her husband's brood of unwound watches,
the marble angel, the Queen Anne chairs,
the porcelain she's never served from, petaled

Tiffany lamps. Unused, the relics shine
like the painter's lily in a jar,
but only while, eyes lit, she says "bronze swan,"
or "jade Buddha," and tells you how it came.

When she gave me a silvery menorah —
one she'd let darken for its vintage glow —
I rubbed it with a cloth, but it went dull
as a shell that's taken from the sea.

I know an elusive master has revealed
her life's design in oils on three wood panels:
a panoply of objects and a gown
the unifying red of her desires.

Last Requests

are clear in books: "Dorset, embrace him . . .
And make me happy in your unity";
and in old movies: "Take care of my hyacinths."
In opera, last pleas fill the diva's arias.

I've waited for last hopes, my amulets
against silence. My father, dying, spoke
in an urgent Polish he'd not used in years,
but his words, staccato trumpet notes,

were not injunctions. When my mother's life
crested like a wave before it breaks,
I asked her wishes. She said, "Ice cream, quick!"
and hurled a glance that said she was not in pain

but dying, and must hurry on with it.
Lips trembled open: "Don't kiss me again.
No, you catch everything. But thanks for coming."
Then quiet. In a trance, a captive audience,

she could not stop my vows, but not a syllable
I uttered had been left unsaid in tiffs,
snarls at ogres in the stories told
on rainy days until the china mugs

rattled on glass shelves, in alphabet games,
nouns binding us like ropes we strung with beads
and lifted up, verbs spinning like bedsheets
we dried, then pulled taut. Words were for wishing

on first daffodils, secrets kept from others.
Now I'll take any edict, fiat, murmur,
gossip, or prayer. Hers, not another's.
When the phone rang at dawn I thought, wrong number,

and blurred the verdict. Even expecting it,
I was not prepared, nor will I be
in her rooms, tapping a crystal bowl,
waiting for words to burn through it like sun.

FROM *For That Day Only* (1994)

For That Day Only

New York, June 11, 1883

Daybreak, and she left her poppyseed roll
to follow them as they walked through the city
carrying the dead child, her fourth brother

born in their new world. Sunlight revealed
a stark, unbending man; a hawklike woman
in a stiff wig, wearing a nubby shawl;

and Uncle Ben, with the bouncing silver watch,
their only kin. Now they exhausted sorrow
by humming sacred phrases in the trek

from Grand Street to the Brooklyn cemetery.
Her mother glanced at her, the oldest daughter,
who had rocked beside the stove and read to him

English words that rang like bits of praise
fallen out of prayer, from Homer's tales
of a nymph whose breath filled sails, images

a storyteller scooped out of a basket
that pierced the morning fog, then disappeared,
like a cat's firecoal eyes — alive, but never

as real as asphalt on this long day.
She never saw the film inside his throat,
and had to be pried away when she tried to breathe

life into his mouth. Just before dawn,
she saw their forms as she sang to the baby's pillow;
hands stroked her hand and led her to the march.

And now, how bright they were. How . . . well, how *visible*.
How steep her father's shoulders. The same light
that warmed them froze gray towers in what was

her first view of the city beyond the neighborhood,
beyond the block. Seeing everything,
trying to see nothing at either side,

she almost smiled at trees, jerked back her head,
remembering herself, and hid her eyes
when she saw a woman speed a bicycle

as though about to rise up over the pavement
like a streetcar's horses that, though ponderous,
might break into a gallop in the wind.

Circles bloomed everywhere: a yellow ball
flew at a hedge; coaches had creaky wheels;
a white hoop, tapped with a stick, zoomed from behind.

There was a brown house with a tulip patch,
for just one family—or so a brass-star
policeman said, who ushered them through crowds

in City Hall Park, and waved at flags on buildings
with plate-glass shop windows. She tripped on loose
cobblestones, and where the streets were roads,

the ground marsh after a night of rain,
she danced and fell, her ankle boots soaked through,
then clambered to the walk to watch a beetle

scurry toward some weeds grown through black gaps
in concrete rectangles. She tried to touch
the statue of a man in bronze that was mottled,

green-going-black, with a beckoning,
historical hand, creased at its great wrist.
Longing to stop by a straw-hat cart near a girl

who tugged at a hatless woman with red real hair,
she pushed on to the harbor, where a gull
barely skimmed her head, and climbed the new

Brooklyn Bridge, her alley to the dead.
Chanting lines of the Psalms to secular tunes
that moved her—local streetcries, arias—

she studied the bearded man in front of her,
observed his set jaw, stirred to his praise,
and feared the tiny boy would grow as heavy

as a bag of stones by the time their journey ended.
Stalwart, proud, he held their grief to his chest
for that day only; moments after sunrise

her mother had raised white arms and yielded up
the shapeless sack. Sun growing higher,
she knew that she, the oldest daughter,

would haul that ragged body even after
the procession ended, when they returned
by gaslight to their dim rooms, and, in fact,

whenever she walked alone in her new city—
brick-hard and vast, but never unredeeming—
the next day and the next one and the next.

The Movie

One day I stumbled on a movie set
Of University Place: a surreal park,
A pointillist mews with gleaming iron gates,
Shuttered buildings hollow at the back,

Streetlights that would topple in a breeze.
Leaving my house, clutching the rubbery basket
I use for farmer's market vegetables,
Gingerly, I walked into a street

Stripped of actual traffic, to discover
"Freshmen" chattering like orioles. A man
In canvas overalls, crowd choreographer,
Barked syllables in opposite directions,

And set us off, a passersby ballet
Whose paths were planned. Some watched for non-existent
Green lights; one woman nervously
Darted, jostling books from pseudo-students.

Then a flower vendor wheeled a wagon
Past us. An actor ran with outstretched arms,
Missed it and cursed it, green eyes so forlorn
I knew that he would follow those geraniums

Forever. And that was all the cameras
Reeled in that morning: one scene with the same
Brightness that had possessed me over the years
I sailed with Bette Davis in a storm

Of black-and-white, trailed Bogart's enemies
Who wear magenta neckties (colorized),
And wept through *Les Enfants du paradis*.
When the director let us go, I realized

That the protection of familiar things
Was limited. At best I was a stranger.
Undoubtedly, the market would be traveling
On wheels to another city, and the copy center

Delivered elsewhere, shelves and window panes.
Some crew would sandblast the "U.S. Government
Post Office" block letters, engraved in stone.
Seeing mica glitter on the pavement,

I scrutinized my neighbors for their real
Identities, and warily questioned every
Role. Under the sun's strobe, at my peril,
I staggered into an enamel sky,

Knowing my destiny would be geraniums,
Blood-red and quivering on a rickety wagon
I might never encounter, only watch them
Drop velvety petals as they rattled on.

The Present Perfect

I saw the cells on TV, as they swam
up to the egg, tails lashing, and I heard
the wind-tunnel sound they make, the steady hum

of thousands, blind, threadlike, worn, but soaring
through waterfalls in their drive to live, move,
and set the egg revolving like a star.

For us, there was no miracle of birth.
No genes, no geniuses. And yet, okay,
we had other things: our work, our history

scrawled on Margaux labels and libretti,
and, after all, no cribs, no sticky plums,
no pulling paper napkins one by one

from a metal box, to mop up dumped ice cream.
But then again, no immortality:
in my religion, children to speak my name

after I am. No heir to your kindness,
your skill with a kite, your father's whimsy,
or to my mother's mother's diamond pin.

And yet we had each other's silences;
freedom to wander with no fixed plan,
now fixed in photos of sylphs that resemble us,

peering down cliffs in Brittany at ragged boards
floated up from dinghies lost at sea,
searching for fish carved into chapels' altars,

spending our suns like out-of-date coins,
until we reached the present-perfect tense—
that have-been state where past and future merge:

we have been married thirty-four years.
I see the kids we were frisk on this lawn
in the late afternoon's unnamable light.

Too late for them, and for their unborn kids,
but not too late for us, here among cedars,
to praise the fires in rose petals on slate;

white rhododendrons, a fountain's rainbow.
I see the dot of you, meadows away,
that grows in sight as you pedal home;

your reddish hair and beard, now tarnished silver,
that once we wanted for a chromosome;
your silhouette in a Manet-like straw hat

as you bless your new astilbe: "Live and be well,"
casting aside your customary questions
for an irrational faith the plant will grow;

I hear your voice that calls me to see wildflowers
poking through gravel cracks in our neighbors' driveway,
slender but fortunate, built to last their day.

Footsteps on Lower Broadway

Grace Church's steeple still fishes the sky
over Broadway, and bobs up from the walker,
Walt Whitman's "lighthouse" on an "inland sea,"
crowded now but unsubmerged by towers,
and seen from building fronts that call up kings:
Renaissance columns, friezes, dormers, bellowing
gargoyles I've missed by never looking up.
I dogged him until his swaggering steps
merged with mine, and I ran into you —
a seething Hungarian immigrant, a Jew.

Hearing "the blab of the pave," I walked from the wharf's
wind-bent sloops and headed for Pfaff's
cave (now haunting a produce stand) to eat
with rowdies and squint at the theater crowd.
I waved at omnibus drivers — Pop Rice, Patsy Dee —
and elbowed by rings of stiff men in black coats
posing like unlighted streetlamps. How he
scowled at their boutonnieres, and touched his beard,
no "washes and razors" for him, nor for you —
an out-of-fashion immigrant, a Jew.

These great houses breathe under their sites.
Gaslight shadows flicker on walls at night.
See the razed opera house on Astor Place
where Badiali sang, and Mario.
For Whitman at St. Ann's, high glorias
blended with deckhands' tunes on the Fulton ferry;
now, drifting under new talk on Broadway,
raw winds carry arias from *Lucia*
that Whitman heard, free-ticketed, and you,
gripping a spear, an immigrant Jew.

Whitman, in a synagogue on Crosby Street,
heard ancient vows in scenes "entirely new."

Men keened, their voices nameless deep-toned bells.
He wrote for the press: a "paneled wood" enclosure
held "sugar loaves" topped with glass and silver;
then, wrapped in white silk, the priest (he *thought*)
waved a parchment scroll. "The heart within
felt awed," he said, and his speech fell
under those minor chords that enchanted you
when you were there, an immigrant, a Jew

who read the Law and knew the ritual.
On Pike Street, where your father was a cantor,
you sang the sacred hymns to melodies
from oratorios you'd heard in concert halls,
and once, a sabbath chant, *Leha dodi*,
"Go, my beloved . . ." to a rollicking tune,
"There's One New York," struck up in a saloon.
Whitman woke to song; you crafted prayer,
whittling down the past to make it new
in your New York, an immigrant, a Jew.

In steamy rain, I zigzagged through your ghetto,
Orchard Street, Hester. Winter-melon bins
replace old pushcarts filled with knives and buttons;
on shop windows, brushstrokes read high to low,
not right-left, as your letters did, and now
graffiti on metal doors are calligraphic.
From here to City Hall you hiked, then on
to Washington Square's law school, looking back
on trees and weed-grown lots—all that you knew
of what was or would be, an immigrant Jew.

Move, move, move, to *con brio* scores
in your head. Praise all things fixed and loose.
Even when you can ride in horse-drawn cars,
walk, to feel unstuck cobbles through your soles,
to see leaves stuck to pebbled rectangles
like jewels in velvet bodices, to peer
from under elms at posters of Irving's *Lear*

and Olga Nethersole's *Camille*. In magic boots
dance on spangled streets that discover you
grateful to be an immigrant, a Jew.

Whitman you neither touched nor read, but here
men and women become one crowd and flow:
shoppers in sweats, kids with shrill radios,
temperance workers, livestock merchants, share
stagecoach clatter, trucks' din, vendors' whines,
and see towers rise: his, slate; yours, marble; mine,
Mondrian's skyscrapers made of the sky.
On misty days, I trek to the port and see
twin water-gazers, he, slouching, and you,
shifting about, a restless immigrant Jew

observing stone cut sharp, cut round: angular
capitals, curved shields; faces of gods.
I gather years carved into stone arcades
and cast on cornices, solid as ancestry,
while I hear a man drum jazz on a kitchen pail.
For Henry James, a walker in your day
you never knew, these streets hummed, bristled, lay
open to change: buildings were words that die
in air; he called them "impudently new"—
as you were then, a prospering immigrant Jew.

I find the Statue of Liberty draped in black
for President Garfield's assassination,
just as you did when your parents packed
in Hungary for free schools. Diamonds shine
in the boat's spume. A castle in the bay!
I've had to shape them, for your past was gone
under new asphalt. Now I hoard stone griffins
and cast-iron numbers, "1 8 7 3,"
on red brick, combing history for you,
Grandfather Dave, an immigrant, a Jew.

New Netherland, 1654

Pardon us for uttering a handful
of words in *any* language, so cut loose
are we from homes, and from His name that is still
nameless, blessed be He. We raised a prayer house—

that is, we broke new wood for one, but some
tough burned it, snarling: "Carve only stones for the dead."
Damp ground, no fire, no psalm we all remember.
But tall ships anchor here, and at low tide,

people with wheat-colored hair look out to sea,
just as we'd searched for land. "Pray if you must,"
my father said, "and when prayer fails, a story,
if it is all you have, will do." Months past,

we left Recife's forced-worship laws in the year
of *their* Lord sixteen hundred and fifty-four, for our new
world, old-country Amsterdam. Leagues seaward,
Spanish pirates slaughtered our scant crew,

and all that was left of us (friends wheezed
their last while they ragged us on) rose up on deck
and tossed our bags in the sea. We watched the wake
turn silver: kiddish wine cups, hanging bowls,

a candelabrum for the promised altar,
carved pointers. Books' pages curled and sank,
prayer shawls ballooned and, soaking, spiraled downward.
Just as we stared, again we heard swords clank—

a French ship, the *Ste. Catherine* (her prow had shone
gold on a gray horizon), came to our
port side and rescued us. In that commotion
on deck, we crouched below—not out of fear,

I swear, but stunned by luminous words
that echoed oddly—beautifully—like lightning
flickering through palls of thickset clouds.
A jaunty captain rasped to us in hiding:

"Where are you bound?"
                        "Amsterdam. Old country."
"Where?"
            "Amsterdam."
                    "Antilles?"
                              "No, Amsterdam."
"Yes, yes. Nieuw *Am*sterdam. I'll see
you get there safely." He meant well, bless him.

Ste. Catherine sailed to land at its tip no larger
than a meadow, fanned out at its sides:
Manhattan Island. Our new master,
Stuyvesant, lashed us with phrases, *wheffs, guzzads,*

that stung but were not fathomed, mercifully,
when we came on a Sabbath, more than twenty
men, women, a baby born at sea.
Still cursing, he let us land, and heard our praise,

then disappeared among lank citizens
with faded skin who stride to the bay and brood
on water that we trust and dread, and listen
to tales unstamped by laws and never sacred.

The Button Box

A sea animal stalked its prey
slithering under her bed, and gorged
on buttons torn from castaways;
ever unsated, it grew large

until it became a deity
spewing out buttons in a fire
of brass for blazers, delft or ruby
for shirts—and dangerous. You'd hear

it snarl when the beds were being made.
It ate stray pins and shot out poison.
But Mother, who stuffed its wooden frame,
scooped up waterfalls of suns,

enamel moons, clocks, cameos,
carved pinwheels, stars, tiny "Giottos,"
peacocks strutting out at sundown,
FDR's profile, flags of Britain,

silver helmets, all with missions.
Mother sewed ballerinas set
in circles on your satin dress,
onyx buttons that would join

you, collar to hood, at graduation;
she would find in the creature's lair
"bones" of an army officer,
"pearls" of a war bride's dressing gown;

nights when the radio hissed *dive bombers,*
Mother dreamed that she could right
the world again by making sure
you had your buttons, sewed on tight.

Site:

The absence of a house. A negative image,
listed at wrong addresses in the guidebooks;
in fact, invisible. Still, it invites
what negative capability the heart

can muster—not simply to observe
the sun's glare on a jet's wing before sunrise,
but in dark rooms to hear a lost friend's laughter.
Take the house at l9 Washington Square,

the one with no brass plaque that claims
it's the site of a house in a book by Henry James.
When the late sun reddens the auburn bricks,
stare until stone steps turn to white marble,

Ionic columns flank the wooden door,
and frayed roses in the yard become
bold peonies restrained by iron fences
handwrought with lyres, Greek frets, acanthus leaves.

Peer through needlepoint lace above a balcony,
and find a woman at a writing table
in a red gown and shawl chosen so "they,
and not she, would look well," and know

that things survive in their sites, in the ghosts of houses,
linger in the incandescent images
of what we imagine has occurred: the parlor
after the guests have gone, the broken phrase

somebody whistled once; the theater's curtain
that holds the mark of the dancer's perilous leap
skyward—the flexed plié, the twist and spin
so high it seemed he would never descend.

Crossing the Square

Squinting through eye-slits in our balaclavas,
we lurch across Washington Square Park
hunched against the wind, two hooded figures
caught in the monochrome, carrying sacks

of fruit, as we've done for years. The frosted, starch-
stiff sycamores make a lean Christmas tree
seem to bulk larger, tilted under the arch
and still lit in three colors. Once in January,

we found a feather here and stuffed the quill
in twigs to recall that jay. The musical fountain
is here, its water gone, a limestone circle
now. Though rap succeeds the bluegrass strains

we've played in it, new praise evokes old sounds.
White branches mimic visions of past storms;
some say they've heard ghosts moan above this ground,
once a potter's field. No two stones are the same,

of course: the drums, the tawny pears we hold,
are old masks for new things. Still, in a world
where fretted houses with façades are leveled
for condominiums, not much has altered

here. At least it's faithful to imagined
views. And, after all, we know the sycamore
will screen the sky in a receding wind.
Now, trekking home through grit that's mounting higher,

faces upturned to test the whirling snow,
in new masks, we whistle to make breath-clouds form
and disappear, and form again, and O,
my love, there's sun in the crook of your arm.

Notes from Underground:
W. H. Auden on the No. 6 Train

Hunched in a corner seat, I'd watch him pass
riders who gaped at headlines: "300 DEAD,"
and, in their prized indifference to all
others, were unaware he was one who heard
meter in that clamor of wheels on rails.

Some days I took the local because he did:
He sank down into plastic, his bruised sandals
no longer straining with the weight of him;
there, with the frankness of the unacquainted,
I studied his face, a sycamore's bark

with lichen poking out of crevices.
His eyes lifted over my tattered copy
of his *Selected Poems*, then up to where
they drilled new windows in the car and found,
I guessed, tea roses and a healing fountain.

All memories are echoes: some whisper,
others roar, as this does. Dazed by war,
I, who winced at thunder, knew that train
screeched "DISASTER!" How it jolted and veered,
station after station, chanting *Kyrie*

eleison, while metal clanged on metal
and bulbs went dim. Peering at tracks, I heard,
"Still persuade us to rejoice." I glimpsed
a worn sandal, turned, and then my eyes
met his eyes that rayed my underworld.

God's Letters

When God thought up the world,
the alphabet letters
whistled in his crown,
where they were engraved
with a pen of fire,
each wanting to begin
the story of Creation.

S said, I am Soul.
I can Shine out
from within your creatures.
God replied, I know that,
but you are Sin, too.

L said, I am Love,
and I brush away malice.
God rejoined, Yes,
but you are Lie,
and falsehood is not
what I had in mind.

P said, I am Praise,
and where there's a celebration,
I Perform
in my Purple coat.
Yes, roared God,
but at the same time,
you are Pessimism—
the other side of Praise.

And so forth.

All the letters
had two sides or more.
None was pure.

There was a clamor
in paradise, words,
syllables, shouting
to be seen and heard
for the glory
of the new heavens and earth.

God fell silent,
wondering,
How can song
rise from that commotion?

Rather than speculate,
God chose B,
who had intoned,
Bashfully, Boldly,
Blessed is *his* name.

And he made A
first in the Alphabet
for admitting, I am All—
a limitation
and a possibility.

Stone Demons

Throw back your head and see them
hunt you down Amsterdam
with pop eyes, knifeblade ears,
gaps weathered into scars,
mouths that cry and drain
waterfalls of rain.

Gargoyles. Bas-reliefs,
worn smooth as buffalo nickels.
And carved beasts — no, not beasts
but pied horrors: animals,
men and women, torn
then tacked together again.

Hear them shriek and owl.
One springs from a cornice,
another squats on a wall,
a third has wings, fishtail,
and hooves, all at once
to fly, swim, leap, and prance.

Cross streets, turn down alleys;
they'll spy you blocks away.
Sages with leafy beards,
kings with fangs, goat ears,
act out court murder scenes
blooded by falling suns.

Hybrid monsters teach us
waking and dreams are one:
our fears, urges, and loves
sit high on towers of sandstone
and poke up from the flat
bedrock of the heart.

False Move

Hearing a thud, as though a ball had struck
my windowpane, seeing a feathery mass
cling to the spot, I peered outside, fearfully
braced for some creature, writhing or inert.

It was a grackle, changing glass to air.
Dead still, the bird was on his feet. Too dazed
to fear my hand, he tilted a stiff head,
opened a knifelike beak but made no sound,

hunched an iridescent back. He's done for:
that polished purple, ebony, and brown
will sink. With glassy eyes, he saw a clearing
larger than his cage of air allowed,

tested its limits, darted as though worlds
could bend. My ground is cumbrous earth that sun
can fire, storms erode. Those silver hills
beyond the hemlocks actually are mountains:

I've scaled their ledges, narrowly escaping
grooves. One step too far, one double image
can kill, I knew, and faltered. Then the bird
lowered his nape, compressed his body, flew.

The Wedding

Late spring in Caesaria, Herod's harbor,
now a city of Roman ruins, quiet
but for gull cries in the white-hot light
of midday. People gather at the shore

as if to see a sword dance, to hear drums
and dagger-beats on shields—the pre-biblical
rites of this region—not the nuptials
of military lovers: agile, slim

army border-guards on active duty
wearing pearl-white wedding costumes, she,
satin and lace, he, linen, stiffly
pressed. Seeming too young to fight or marry,

they pose for photographs, the sea exploding
on rocks, and, shoes cast off, run on hot sand
to the marriage canopy, a covering
to cast off demons. It snaps in high wind,

their sacred roof, a dazzling cotton
embroidered prayer shawl whose supporting poles
are rifles held by three men and a woman
in combat fatigues. There, before them all,

a rabbi intones the seven benedictions,
offers wine, hears vows and blesses them,
and blesses children who sing psalms. At sundown,
when the bridal pair change into uniforms,

a shot rings out. A woman screams and falls.
Three of the groom's attendants grab the rifles
that held the canopy, fall to the ground
at the stammer of guns, rub faces with wet sand,

and, shouldering their weapons, run to the sea,
firing at men who creep out of a dinghy
that's dragged aground. One of the intruders,
his buoyant gait so like the bride's

that he seems an invited cousin, drops to the shore,
face down. Another stranger staggers
a few yards, bleeding, his stubby fingers
frozen on his gun. Bodies pitch forward,

arms and legs flail. Silence. White garments strewn
like a book's blown pages, the groom bends down
to lift the prayer shawl that lies, torn,
mud-splattered. He folds it, kisses it, then

flings his red beret to the darkening
sand. Leading his bride to a small car,
he turns back for a time, as though to hear,
through mounting wave sounds, what the children sang.

Julian of Norwich

Warped in the window-diamonds of my cell,
distorted, outsize primroses unfold:
I see all manner of things that shall be well.

Eyeless men with plague-sores come to chapel,
hungry, with blood-soaked poultices, and cold.
Warped in the window-diamonds of my cell,

they lurch and fall, inert. Another dead bell.
Their king gone, my King blesses (dressed in gold,
I see) all manner of things that shall be well.

Hermits recoil. If I were to foretell
doom, monks would believe. Instead, I'm called
warped. In the window-diamonds of my cell

are men who know Black Death and wars, and tell
of starless night, and will until I'm old,
I see. All manner of things that shall be well

deceive: dense glass in quarrel panes can spell
disaster, lunacy. Faces are bold,
warped in the window-diamonds of my cell.
I see all manner of things that shall be well.

Rescue in Pescallo

Neither do I believe in miracles,
although at times an actual homely image
can lift the eyes and the expectations. Pale,
dark-haired, severe, a woman from the village

of Pescallo said a statue of Christ
had washed up on these shores and startled schoolboys,
who called some local men, fishing for trout.
They listened closely, as for a drowned man's cries

of life, and stared at the figure, carved in oak,
the body painted white, the hair and beard
black. They hauled it up and carried it
to the Church of San Giacomo, a good

kilometer away, where she'd last seen it, lying
under a fresco of the Deposition
ascribed to Perugino. "Now the painting
may well be a replica, but that wooden

figure is unique, for what it is,"
she said, and frowned. "You know the yellow-white
scant flower, the anemone? It grows
among these stones, in shade. So too that

carving bobbed on the waves and steered through ice.
I guess it came as flotsam, possibly
junked, along with boards that had been pews,
cast out of a ruined chapel in a nearby

harbor on the lake." Rapt, she continued,
"Or, perhaps, in transit, it fell overboard,
not to be retrieved until, by God,
it loomed up here." The woman halted, stirred

by some dark memory, and threw a tarpaulin
over her stone sarcophagus. A sculptor
who modeled snaky forms, her studio once
a stable on a villa near the water,

she led me down an aisle of cypresses
that trapped a cloud, and would, until the wind
rose. It seemed we glided in a tapestry
of towers and doves, all things enlarged beyond

normal scale in the clear air. I gathered
the statue baffled her. She dismissed events
that wanted proof, and knew the dense-grained wood,
the size and weight, the tides, the precise moment

it surfaced, but she inferred that it had come
—like penstrokes in her drawings for sarcophagi—
from a chillier place than she could fathom,
try as she did. Returning to the story,

she said, "That day, the south wind we call *breva*
brought ghostly mist that dimmed the bald horizon,
welding sky and water into metal.
In fog, the people saw the mud-smirched, lean

Christ walk through their spiraling thin streets,
hoisted on the shoulders of two fishermen,
staggering, really, head, nailed feet, and torso
one seesaw plank that passed the shops, the one

waterfront caffè, and the pier. It sidled
onto the Via Garibaldi, where
it nearly grazed a bench when one man buckled
and fell. Seeing the statue waver

and lean a bit, clerks left their shops, doors open,
to set it right. Determined carabinieri,
who'd seen the pallid relic pass their station
in mist, stopped traffic. Blank-faced passersby

joined a kind of ritual parade that went
to the church door, where nuns and merchants set
the mottled body, scrubbed, dabbed with new paint,
on a slab inside the crypt." The woman thought

none of the villagers knew what had happened,
in their minds' eyes, or were the better for it.
"They're all retarded cousins in Pescallo,"
she muttered to her watch, an hour late.

She had shunned Daylight Time, since, as a girl,
she heard Il Duce rule it into law;
she doubted love, distrusted friendship, grateful
simply to look, bear witness, and withdraw.

Charcoal-haired, with eyes both fixed and empty,
and moon-blanched skin, she carved heads in the style
of Donatello, then, in Milan, she woke
to obscure archbishops' tombs in purple

marble, amazed at life flesh-eaters gave,
and made sarcophagus relief. Tenaciously,
she chiseled Hindu deities, brave
princes and governors in vaults. Not airy

avatars but weighty men and women
danced on her coffins. Curiously, they changed,
each more itself when its contours were gone
to others in the clusters she arranged.

Finishing one sculpture, then another,
she ticked off years, then bent under great losses.
Lifeless as crystal, she intoned that after
her son had died of leukemia in Venice,

her husband gone, she felt her own life flicker.
Somehow her forms assumed finer detail,

although she noticed actual things grow weaker,
their outlines vague. Searching for new soil,

she wandered to this country, where she saw,
in early spring, a branch of apricot
in bloom among stiff twigs. A week of sun
had undone heavy frost, and startled it.

Seeing the terraced valley, where small houses
were terra-cotta rectangles that shone
through haze, near ancient olive trees and fortresses,
she set about to cut resistant limestone

and red marble to life in the sarcophagi,
visions of tombs for her imagined kings;
she cut them into birth as unexpectedly
as violets spring from rock. "People and things

existed for me here in fabulous harmony,
so natural it seemed strange. Although the white
citrus trees and pines covered the land,
chapels and piers were never out of sight."

She smoothed a canvas skirt, her mica eyes
fastened on snow-covered mountain peaks. The task
of creating angular deities in friezes
was good. But still, occasionally, at dusk,

she said, she watched the steamboat from Varenna
furrow the lake, and hurried to the landing
to meet the boy whose death she'd dulled away
in those gray moments. She shuddered, recalling

sunsets obscured by vapor. "Only the chirr
of motors told me where I was. Mist fell,
and dimmed out the eroded planks, the pier's
geometry, lake scum, the rotted guardrail.

Fog beckoned me. And also, as the south wind
moves, I brought an inner mist that blurred
or made my universe, although the mind
saved clearness for the work. One day I heard

San Giacomo's bells before I reached the wharf.
Purchasing wine and olives in a store,
I faltered; then, for all I scorned belief
(it was at vespers), I tugged at the door."

Cautious as a night marauder, stranger
to her first house, she stepped gingerly
behind bowed shoulders, found a bench, and glanced
at the bone-white relic washed ashore and quietly

repaired, the soggy belly bleached, the pupils
glossed. Perhaps a craftsman from Bellano
modeled the piece some eighty years before,
and, after he finished, saw wood glow.

Her neighbors had renewed the harrowed image
that survived somehow. "Yes, a miracle,"
she said aloud, and halted at the one
word that meant too much, explained too little.

Watching a carpenter from Bergamo
turn to regard the idol he had planed,
she saw at last her own figures as metaphors,
more alive than men, more dead than stone.

There, as the north wind rose up in the mountains,
she knew the statue held fast just as limestone
and marble tombs are genuine. But then,
unlike those sculptures, her mortal son

was of a transient brightness, and could never
return or be restored. Without repeating

those random thoughts, she never searched the pier
again for the dead child. Her story ending,

I knew volcanic tremors had ripped open
her eyes when that zinc-white log floated up here.
Her voice was fathoms down when she asserted,
"Christ rose on these shores, eleven years

ago, and on this day, the eve of Tenebrae
— the holy litany of gathering shadows —
this last week of Lent, before Good Friday
and the Great Vigil." Nodding at a yellow

primrose, she measured days as kilos verify
an infant's being, then said she saw light flare
through clouds long after dusk. She turned to me,
knowing I understood her words, and, more,

the truth of radiant images that rise,
unbidden, from the bottom of the mind's
dark waters, to survive whirlpools and surface,
mud-soaked, tattered, worn, to beach on sand,

bodiless, lake-drenched carriers of keenest
vision, loosened, when given legs and heads,
to clarify the mist, just as she freed
souls of those whose bodies she had made.

El Greco's *Saint James, the Less*

This moonlight fractured into mere threads of stars
shines now on eyes indifferent or turned to some
    white peak inside that none but he sees,
  he, and those taught by the painter's vision.

Light falls on blue-and-red robes whose shadows are
black mouths that cry of glare that has deepened them.
    One hand unfurls; its lambent fingers
  curve down, then curl up, a torch upended.

That hand recalls a starburst that hung from a
white pine; it turned in altering light, and its
    green needles fell away and pointed at
  random, a fan on its branch, an uncertain omen.

One day a mourning dove that was stammering
faint notes flew low, splayed out like the tangle of
    white pine. The bird, the tree, and now that
  hand of Saint James are one form. The dove gone,

light stays, its glow the mind's brightness, gleam of a
first day on earth in tales of Creation when
    one beam that God devised, before the
  sun, would have shown us the world in one glance.

Carrion

The chipmunk's carcass lay flat on a stone
stair that led to rooms above the shed.
Hind legs, a tail, a strand of wine-red beads
and innards, showed whose body it had been.

One step above the corpse, a cat discreetly
unfurled, with eyes half closed, guarding the kill.
Caretakers had fed him well, and still
the animal had craved some swifter prey.

The cat himself, ill-used, had been abandoned.
Boarded at stables here to calm the horses,
he was released after the racing season
passed, and found a temporary place

on this estate. Later, he would be free
to forage in the woods. The horse he eased
"will make a good brood mare when her racing days
are done," the auctioneer said. Rings of grief:

Scissors, paper, rock, I sang as a child.
Scissors cuts paper that covers rock
that pulverizes scissors. Still I'm locked
in that small circle, flaying, being flayed.

Small fingers whipped my wrist: bland-mannered Catherine
was *paper*. I, being *rock*, would lash
my dearest Ann, with flimsy yellow hair,
for being *scissors*. So the wheel turned, and turns.

I touched the chipmunk's glittering cadaver,
then buried it. The cat quivered to stand,
warning my hand that stole the prize he murdered.
Beyond the steps, a spruce raised votive candles.

Walking through double rows of junipers
that day, I glanced away from cruelty,
or so I tried: a hawk warped in midair
called back the day I watched a herring gull

circle to land, scoop up a turtle, glide
upward again, and drop it to crack its shell.
My neighbor shot the gardener who denied
he ever cared, and who was seen at Bill's

drinking bourbon with a new lover.
"She seemed too old, too stoical, for murder.
She won't get off," a villager asserted —
sadly, I thought. I never knew the killer,

had seen her only, taut as a dry leaf
someone had kicked on the ground, chilly, slight,
her skin worn porcelain, her long body
angular in stride, flexed, as in flight.

That night my feet, my elongated thighs,
stiffened and went cold; then, as I lay
counting the stars, my carrion entrails
flickered below my eaten chest, my eyes.

The Good Women

The Luxembourg Gardens

Who caught them this way? Shapely stone
queens and other *grandes dames* lurk in trees,
cousins to the Statue of Liberty,
another classy vamp. They are made of contradiction:

Geneviève, a saint whose prayers saved Paris
from the invader, clenches her long fingers,
and peers through leaves,
                       round bosom, snaky braids;

Queen Matilda, Duchess of Normandy,
of the sword and crown, the cross and the fleur-de-lis,
rests the tall sword
                       against a narrow waist.

Waving a scepter, Queen Blanche of Castille,
who rescued the kingdom from rebels,
frees one hand
                       to clutch a billowing skirt,

while Charlemagne's mother, Bertha of the Great
Feet, holds her king, Pepin the Short,
and his throne
                       in her unsceptered hand

near fierce Queen Margaret of Anjou,
"She-wolf of France, and worse than wolves of France,"
who glides,
                       clasping her son to a curvy bodice,

and there is Hugo de Sade's wife, Laura de Noves,
possibly Petrarch's bold (here reticent) love,

beside Clémence Isaure,
                              who leans on one hip.

Under a wide-eyed Louise de Savoy,
who, not so simply, joined another queen
to arrange a peace treaty of Cambrai.
I slide into an iron chair, and frown

at an unseemly décolletage
some Beaux Arts sculptor dreamed had been the rage,
wrong, or at the least, chilly for court.
Then, as I leave, I watch a girl spell out:

"M-A-R-G-U-E-R-I-T-E D-E F-R-A-N-C-E," Margaret
of Angoulême, queen of Navarre, who wrote
tales that inspired Rabelais, and here—
(one hand touches the cheek, the other holds flowers)

coquette—allays my doubts: all oxymorons,
saints, muses, consorts, sages, scholars,
mothers of, daughters of, sirens, leaders,
flame up in paradox—those are the queens.

FROM *Hemispheres* (1984)

Blessed Is the Light

Blessed is the light that turns to fire, and blessed the flames
    fire makes of what it burns.
Blessed the inexhaustible sun, for it feeds the moon that shines
    but does not burn.
Praised be hot vapors in earth's crust, for they force up
    mountains that explode as molten rock and cool, like love
    remembered.
Holy is the sun that strikes the sea, for surely as water burns
    life and death are one. Holy the sun, maker of change, as
    it melts ice into water that lessens mountains, hones peaks
    and carves gullies.
Sacred is the mountain that crumbles over time. Jagged peaks
    promise permanence but change, planed by rock-slides, cut
    by avalanche, crushed, eroded, leached of minerals.
Behold the arcs your eyes make when you speak. Behold the
    hands, white fire. Branches of pine, holding votive candles,
    they command, disturbed by wind, the fire that sings in me.
Blessed is whatever alters, turns, revolves, just as the gods
    move when the mind moves them.
Praised be the body, our bodies, that lie down and open and
    rise, falling in flame.

Let There Be Translators!

> "And the Lord said, 'Behold, the people is one and they have all one language . . . Go to, let us go down, and there confuse their language, that they may not understand one another's speech.'"
> —Genesis xi: 6, 7.

When God confused our languages, he uttered,
in sapphire tones: "Let there be translators!"
And there were conjurors and necromancers
and alchemists, but they did not suffice:
they turned trees into emeralds, pools to seas.

God spoke again: "Let there be carpenters
who fasten edges, caulk the seams, splice timbers."
They were good.
                    God said: "Blessed is the builder
who leaves his tower, turns from bricks and mortar
to marvel at the flames, the smith who fumbles
for prongs, wields andirons, and prods live coals,
who stokes the hearth and welds two irons as one."

Praised was the man who wrote his name in other
handwriting, who spoke in other tones,
who, knowing elms, imagined ceiba trees
and cypresses as though they were his own,
finding new music in each limitation.

Holy the one who lost his speech to others,
subdued his pen, resigned his failing sight
to change through fire's change, until he saw
earth's own fire, the radiant rock of words.

Sutton Hoo Ship Burial

> *In the British Museum are objects belonging to a 7th century Anglo-Saxon king, which were found in August 1939 in the remains of a boat at Sutton Hoo, on Suffolk's River Deben, near the North Sea.*

He rose out of the sea, the last warrior,
months before Dunkirk, days before invasion,
not his remains, but things: a boar's-head brooch;
epaulets, coins; a six-stringed willow harp;
christening spoons beside an auroch's horn.
His helmet found, the absent king endured,
his house battered by water; and as water

turns to ice and kills, it broke the hull,
scattering narrow strakes that marked the sand,
nailprints; but the hull would give life back again
as snails plunge into earth before the spring—
a resurrection shell; so he appeared,
beached among swamp ferns fronded in the bog,
monarchs of nests and ruler of enclosures.

He may have been the real Beowulf,
beekeeper, guardian of law. He fought nightmares,
not men: he conquered trolls and firedragons
and slew Cain's sons, sea monsters, keeping peace
within himself, dreading the heart's Grendels
that brought invaders, past and future wars,
Danelaw that split the kingdom, killing men.

Weeks before lightning war, and the sea blockades,
a woman found the last warrior's bark;
his body lay in heath covered by bracken.
A pagan ship, a Christian burial
in holy ground for a king who sanctified
God and the gods. Not his remains but things
would sail him to the next world as a king.

Ring-giver, father of swords, of artisans,
emerging, moving toward me in the night,
he brings me dreams of refuge in a shell.
I see his shadow now, for I hear my past
in my body's shell, in reveries of almonds.
As he loomed out of the sea to tell his story
of mud-drenched creatures in the mind's black waters

who thrashed ungoverned ghosts at the sea's edge,
I find my house in a stone, my world in acorns,
my solitude in galleys holding bowls,
bronze stags, gold buckles, swords inlaid with garnets,
stars locked in hollows, hidden and revealed.
In rocks I will know eels and sea-anemones
before I surface into murderous air.

Morning Song

Norwegian spruce trees, veering to red-brown.
You are asleep, your body cool as dawn.
As I turn to leave, sun strikes the terrace,
affirming day. Amazed, through junipers,
my eyes raise watchmen on the mansion tower.
Our clothes will spin together in the laundromat:
doomed lovers circle, drifting on the winds.

The Stars and the Moon

> *In* Legends of the Jews, *Lewis Ginzberg writes that an Egyptian princess hung a tapestry woven with diamonds and pearls above King Solomon's bed. When the king wanted to rise, he thought he saw stars and, believing it was night, slept on.*

Scaling ladders with buckets of white enamel,
I painted the stars and the moon on my windowpanes
to hold back days and nights. I yanked the telephone
and stopped the wooden clock. The weeks a lightning stroke,
desire turned to love. With my blue diamond,
I sliced minutes in half and made days vanish,
fooling the hours.

                        I became so skillful
at firmaments that miracles occurred:
a bearded comet moved across the room
breeding no omens, tearing no major kingdoms
into small provinces, but there it was,
reminding us that rock may spin and flare,
lifting the senses, burning into sight.

You eased pale hands away; I saw your shoulders
recede through doorways, watched your image fail
with your famished smile. I left our room
with dream-filled eyes, and standing in the sun,
I gazed at bricks and glass and saw, suddenly,
flashing in stony light, the stars and the moon.

The Flight

That day I hired a private detective to follow me,
and could not read his notes. In a tangled grove,
I hid behind white pines, compressed my body,
then watched him write, left-handed and myopic,
under an Irish cap, when I asked for help
from strangers who spoke Slavic languages.
Wary, moving ahead, I found a depot,
watched an immense train churn, haloed in steam,
and boarded, second class. I had no ticket,
and my expired passport represented
a drooping head with unfamiliar eyes.
Unshaken, rows behind, the stranger waited,
wielding camera and pen. Across the border
I disembarked, but knew he would capture me,
with soundless footsteps, even on black gravel.

I tried to recall my crime. I know I am guilty,
but never why. Lawless, I have ignored
those signs: WRONG WAY: GO BACK and NO WAY OUT,
circles that tell me YOU ARE HERE. I gather
it is the whispers that explode, the looks
that make dogs whimper. When I bow in prayer
I think of love; I know I've killed my friends,
pelting them with a touch — and yet I've heard
they are alive. Besides, that's not the real
offense. I would cross any path, or trek
through swamps to find my crime. But even he,
that bald, insistent man who follows me,
unsleeping, cannot tell me what I've done.

FROM *Burn Down the Icons* (1976)

The Abbess of Whitby

There must have been an angel at his ear
When Caedmon gathered up his praise and sang,
Trembling in a barn, of the beginning,
Startled at words he never knew were there.

I heard a voice strike thunder in the air:
Of many kings, only one god is king!
There must have been an angel at his ear
When Caedmon gathered up his praise and sang.

When Caedmon turned in fear from songs of war,
Gleemen who sang the glories of the king
And holy men wondered that so great a power
Could whirl in darkness and force up his song;
There must have been an angel at his ear
When Caedmon gathered up his praise and sang.

Written on a Road Map

This chapel stands between Morgan and Dol
Inside the gargoyle's head of Brittany
Where towns are pale gray names and roads are numbers;
Nameless, deserted; it is closed for August.

But how the shadows of a Calvary
Flicker like puppets managed by the sun;
In the yard, a soldier's name is cut on stone,
His life, in numbers, and a word, *Regrets*.

Barbara of the storm, John of the sea,
Saint Catherine fix me here, your fire my fire,
Establishing a chapel on a map
To stop the blur of trees, the flow of roads.

Names

"This is ozone," you said,
staring at absolute air,
startled by all things
palpable, familiar;
the less we know
about a thing, the more
names we give it.
Nominal friend,
I find you in rain,
see you in waves that radiate
rainbows,
your voice inventing
hemlocks, rose-breasted
grosbeaks. Even now,
this weedy grove spins
starflowers, arbor-
vitae, aspens,
and foamflowers
(one word);
from the bottom
of your word-hoard,
names order the world.

Street Dance in Barcelona

Alone, I watched the solemn dance begin,
Waking from a silence that deceives,
That turns footsteps, or the rustle of dry leaves
Into the clatter of a tambourine.

Their voices had been rattling that day,
Rapid as drumbeats, in the Catalan,
But a wilderness of hands reached toward the sun
Like wheatstalks risen from a ground of clay.

The crowd broke into perfect wheels, turning
To the stuttering of a wooden horn,
Quickened by the beating of the sun;
I had seen their angry faces burning.

Strangers, we stand alone but turn together
As vanes become a windmill in the wind;
One hand opens for another hand,
The wheel breaks only to include another.

Surely as Certainty Changes

Surely as certainty changes,
As tide moves sand,
As heat sends wind to force the sea into waves,
As water rises and returns in rain
Or circles into smoke and falls in vapor,
You are enchanted for you enter change
And change is holy.

As earth's weight compresses rocks
Under trees over time, you enter change,
I know your face gives light as I know fire
Alters everything,
And falls rising,
Feeds and nourishes, opens and closes.

I pray to Proteus, the god of change
And proteolysis, "the end of change
Changing in the end;"
To break old images and make you new
As love is its own effect unendingly.

Poetry Editor

Caught on a traffic island
in Park Avenue, I waited,
staring at dahlias,
cars enclosing me in a moving
parenthesis, red lights
arresting me. The stranger came,
wary, lizardlike, observing me
observe him, pressing pages
in my hand: "I want to talk with you
about matters of interest
to both — my poetry."
                              "Of course."

From a drawer with grooves
for silver needles, my dentist
reached for metaphors.
                       "Oh yes,
of course."

            And when my neighbor
at a farmhouse in the pines
lodged notes he thought I had not seen
beneath my breakfast plate, I said again,
"Of course."

Day of Atonement: in the house of God
trumpets began an elusive,
uncertain staccato flourish;
then, the horn stuttered
that once woke me
to song: "Let mountains rise
to trumpets throughout the land."
Trembling to that blare, I saw
a choir angel flutter
a white arm that implored me

to hear his cadences.
Wavering, I whispered,
"Of course."

      And yet again
of course. For, day by day, those images
rise like smoke, turn like a windmill,
furnish a beehive
I have not arranged; I never know
when fire in some unlikely place
will seize me; when my ears will reel
to that elusive music.

      Worn at last,
I flew to Antibes and, one day,
swimming toward me
under a snorkel,
a masked man cried *"Attends!"*
his manuscript translated
into English, lying
on black stones.

      "Bien sûr," I said,
as on the traffic island.
I, too, look for mail.
And when green signals tell me to, I cross
Park Avenue,
waiting for a comet
to flare suddenly,
firing
my landscape
of bricks and glass.

The Examination: Remembrance of Words Lost

—What happened at your orals, Grace?
Taking a pipe from a row of suckling pigs, the chairman swung
In his chair. An A-shaped face, kind voice. Eyes, rubber stamps:
Failure. Special case.

              —I lose it now,
But I will try to call it back. Dim stars
That fade to a stare can shine at a backward glance.

—Why did you fail?

              —I did not. Words failed *me*
When I heard words about words, and swallowed tides
Of questions, as rock-hollows suck sea.

—Why are you here?

              —A star once summoned me,
As gravity pulls others to the ground.
That star is light-years distant from me now,
But still it burns, unseen, waiting to shine.
I wait for syllables to fall. Or burn, like ice.

—Good answer, though your style is hard to follow.
These numbers: Ninety percent of you are brainless,
My records show, though eighty-six percent
Pass on the second try. But you—good teacher,
Student, lover of words. What happened, Grace?

—They led me to a room with a womb-shaped table
On which my fathers laid twelve hands. Six scraped faces nodded.
Above, fluorescent rectangles were frozen lakes
Of corrugated glass. The walls were soundproof.
I greeted a darning-egg.

                      —We haven't met
Officially.

           Mist fell. Tide went over me.

—In eighteen-eighty, where would you buy a book?

—At the corner of Third and Bleecker, in ribs of sun,
Where I left my mind.

                    Their voices bonged
Contrapuntally:

                  —The chicken or Emily Dickinson?
The egg enjoined. Another:

               —Stephen or Hart?
Henry or William? I did not know
Which of his heads to answer. Totem pole
Of painted masks gone white.

A man with a face like a dime on edge said,
Fields away,

            —Was there a real
House in Albany? His headlights caught my eyes.

There was. I lived there once. But I can't recall
Where Henry was when William was at Harvard.

Their voices thrummed:

            —Internal evidence?
                —Any sex
In Sextus Propertius?

           —Elders, let me finish
Bathing. I am no exhibitionist.

When Caedmon turned from song to sing
Hild made him monk, but only after
God made him poet—and I think his God
Was some dark fierce power that forced up his song.
I cannot tell you how he sang, how syllables
Danced from a man who could not read.

        —A monk?
Oh, yes. Of course. But nowadays we can't
Give Ph.D.s for *that*. What's your profession?

—Poet.

    —Published poet?

      —Yes.

        —Well, *poetry*
Has nothing to *do* with scholarship. Your sentence:
A year of failure and a crown of silence.

Five fathers vanished. One remained.

      —My friend,
I see you have been walking under water.
Look upward now.

       I surfaced then, saw shadows
That had been knives, and moved into myself.

In the Country of Urgency, There Is a Language

To Marianne Moore

> *"Ezra Pound said never, NEVER to use
> any word you would not actually say in
> moments of utmost urgency."*

1

"Can you hear me? I talk slowly now,"
You said, months past. "When Ezra Pound
Came, he could not say a word."
When your voice waned, I prodded syllables,
Examined frequencies, listened for cadences,
Demanding clarity. Sounds inconceivable
Have meaning now. Four heavy stresses:
"How is your work?" Light syllables:
"Do I look well?" Fire-forced speech
Caught, wordless. It will suffice.

2
December 22, 1970

In the country of urgency, there is a language
I hear as I follow the fall of your hand
And a blue light from the door of your dark apartment.
Your body vanishes behind bedrails.
Your hand I can't let go flows into me.

Blue eyes burn images in me. Those images,
Those sounds, those necessary gestures
Are a language. They will suffice.

3
                                          September 17, 1969

No note from you. Remembering your leopard,
"Spotted underneath and on its toes,"
And how you'd said, "a leopard isn't spotted
Underneath, but in the tapestries it is,
And I liked the idea," I brought the photograph
Of leopards spotted everywhere. Home from the hospital,
Immobile, in a billowing blue gown,
You stalked those beasts and raised yourself in bed:
"Those are cheetahs, Grace!" and lay down again.

4

Your silence is a terrible fire in me that sings on to be fed,
A musical wind that splits my craft, hail-hard, that lashes me dumb.
It is a strange country. Where are the maps,
The lighthouses, the gyroscope you gave me
That rights itself in motion? I have forgotten my name
As well as the irregular conjugations I memorized.
Occasionally, though, a blue light flashes directions
Over dangerous shale, and I hear you
Over protest shouts, explosions, immolations,
Over unreliable telephone connections, I hear you
Over labels, over a broken air conditioner, a plane;
I hear you over the silences we call conversation.
Your voice rolls in me thunder in a night of invisible stars,
And I wake to the sounds of your silence. They are a language.
      They will suffice.

Burn Down the Icons

What happened to Cassandra? She who cried
In me "Love is war!" has died, loving.
And Daphne, whose flesh grew leaves?
Breasts now, and twig-shaped nerves.
Father, forgive me. It had to be.
I never promised to be Saint Veronica
When you pressed images on me, printed in blood
On a white scarf. Or when you carved me in marble,
And gazed into the dry wells of my eyes,
Did you think I would not dissolve?

Well, burn down the icons. I have moved
Out of the Prado. Your best fresco
Cracks from the ceiling. I have gone
Beyond my body, five feet eleven and three-quarters
Inches of tangled philodendron. I am water.

Call out the curia. Unsanctify me.
Erase my feast day from the calendar.
Shatter the stained-glass windows of my mind.
They were idolaters who cut the palm,
Two anchors and an arrow on my tomb
Found in the catacombs. I am no martyr.

Love was my habit. I know my heart moved trees.
Love called my eyes to change things of this world.
But I did not believe it. And how could I persuade you
That those visions you admired were astigmatism.
Makers of images, what you created in me
I was. But see me new! My nipples are cathedrals,
My flesh is a miracle. I flow to the ocean
Where all the rivers of the earth come together.
My body is a holy vessel. I am fire and air.

Do not desert me now, although I pray

To a genital god, and have let blaze
Strange images, my means of transportation.
I have established my chapel in water.
I would move through mountains. But fathers,
Let me return to a safe harbor; like the waves'
Slate-sheets, crash in the jetties of your arms.

Letter to Helen

For Dr. Helena Waldman-Gold, 1898-1943

1

Your face broods from a sepia photograph:
Eyes light over cheekbones.
Helen, I cannot lose your indelible
name, although I lose
others of the time.
When acts burn, there are images,
icons of blood and sweat
printed on my mind.

I have to recreate
your deed from rumors
in the quick ears
of the child I was, from Black Books
I was allowed *not* to read. I have to guess
you knew our law of invisible
light: "Therefore choose life
that thou and thy seed shall live."
We dance to songs
in a world below ice, below time,
sleepwalk to laws
that manage our acts. Living our law
and science, your faith,
condemned to die,
you leaped from a tower in Poland, your death
firing our lives.

2

For years I would lessen your nobility,
call it impulsive, plead

it was useless, say
the sudden splendid act is no great thing,
survival is; the steady patient choice
of rightness over time, and excellence —
patience, the hero's passion.

To yield is to come back, I said, as water
yields to cleave stone, as tide ebbs
to move shorelines. Awakening at last
in a strange country, sun-dazed, I knew
the world's calm when acts
are stilled. Storms coned inward,
I stared down wind that spirals to an eye,
and knew I was the heart of the storm,
born of the same that war is born.
"Therefore choose life," I cried, for David wept
when Absalom was slain, his criminal,
his outlaw son, however hard
the King had danced before God,
the ark safe in Jerusalem.

3

A transatlantic call, beamed from a satellite:
I asked him, "Will you say
Celan's *'Fadensonnen'*? I cannot find
your version." Static then,
and speech with echoes: "'there are
still songs to be sung . . . sung . . . sung . . .
on the far side
of mankind . . . kind . . . kind.'
Damn that echo!"
My friend, your quiet voice insists on peace
like *Dona nobis pacem*, in an antiphonal
high mass with fuguelike shadows.

4

Blood forces up my praise.
I am a fountain, juggling blades
to God, while everywhere the dead
lie on the streets, in crevasses, in fields;
today a woman set herself on fire,
her body charred, her flesh burned to a log,
fire flattened her mouth and slit her eyes.

Fire forces me. I shout my praise
to the other side of humankind,
my name a blue number burned
on forearms of the imagination.
Your name was, is, will be, Helen.
And you will come for years, salamander,
name of fire and unharmed by fire.
That is what icons are, indelible
prints on the mind. Your image is a fresco
that will not come down
in dust. Because you lived your life I shine
in flames, burning but not consumed,
changing to be myself, as though if water burned
it would be water all the more.
Courage you gave me, Helen, and your name
draws me like fire.

Notes

The Marble Bed

MOMENT IN RAPALLO (page 44). Phrases in italics are from "A Retrospect," "How to Read," and "The ABC of Reading," by Ezra Pound. "An old scribe quotes King Solomon." From the Midrash Tehillim.

ALIVE AND WELL: TOMB SCULPTURES IN THE STAGLIENO CEMETERY (page 46). "Angel," for tomb of Francesco Oneto (1882) by sculptor Giulio Monteverde; "Widow," for Pienovi (1879) by Giovanni Battista Villa (1832–1899); "Dreamer," for Carlo Erba (1883) by Santo Saccomanno (1833–1914); "Maria Francsca," for Delmas (1909) by Luigi Orengo (1865–1940). She died young, 1909, in an auto accident. "Struggle" for Celle (1891–93) by Giulio Monteverde (1837–1919). And "Woman in Sunlight" (1920) by Enrico Pacciani Formari (1996–1858).

DR. JOHN (page 57). Stage name of Malcom John Rebennack, Jr.

Without a Claim

WITHOUT A CLAIM (page 71). The Montauk chief is Wyandanch, also known as Wyandance and Wyandank. For details about the Montauks here and elsewhere in my poems, I am grateful to *The Montauket Indians of Eastern Long Island,* by John A. Strong; *Men's Lives,* by Peter Matthiessen; *Springs: A Celebration,* by Ken Robbins and Bill Strachan; and *Hampton's Bohemia,* edited by Constance Ayers Denne and Helen Harrison.

WOMAN ON THE CEILING (page 80). Seen in an exhibit called "Images of Christ," at New York University's Institute for the Study of the Ancient World, in the autumn of 2011.

SHADOW (page 91). Miles Davis and Juliette Gréco.

YELLOW (page 92). In the early 1960s, Chris Albertson traveled from Denmark to find jazz artists in the South and feature them on recordings for Riverside Records.

GREEN RIVER (page 102). Artists and village workers lie in this cemetery, on Accabonic Road, East Hampton, New York

TATTOO (page 104). "Let your chosen objective . . ." attributed to Wei T'ai, an eleventh-century Chinese poet.

The Broken String

THE BROKEN STRING (page 107). Itzhak Perlman's performance of Mendelssohn's Violin Concerto took place at Avery Fisher Hall in New York on November 18, 1995. The story of the broken string was reported in the *Houston Chronicle*, February 10, 2001.

BLUE IN GREEN (page 115). Miles Davis, trumpet; John Coltrane, tenor, in *Kind of Blue*.

KOL NIDREI, SEPTEMBER 2001 (page 117). The attack on September 11 preceded by only sixteen days the chanting of Kol Nidrei ("All Vows") on Yom Kippur, a high holiday in Judaism. Its ritual enacts a legal plea to cancel all promises made in the preceding year and in the year to come.

ART TATUM AT THE GEE-HAW STABLES (page 121). I'm grateful for *Too Marvelous for Words: The Life and Genius of Art Tatum*, by James Lester.

THE HORROR (page 122). Details of Chaim Soutine's life from *Soutine*, by Monroe Wheeler (Museum of Modern Art, 1950) and "Abstracting Soutine," by Arthur C. Danto, *The Nation*, August 24/31, 1998.

DEATH (page 124). Second-line beat. In a traditional New Orleans jazz funeral, the band swings into improvisational jazz, but only after they have played Christian hymns from church to cemetery. Leaving the burial, at a respectful distance, the lead trumpeter sounds a two-note riff and the drummers roll out the second-line. In *Rejoice When You Die: The New Orleans Jazz Funerals,* by Vernal Bagneris, photographs by Leo Touchet. Also, Louis Armstrong talks of the second-line in an Edward R. Murrow documentary, *Satchmo the Great*. Passages in italics are my translations of *Beowulf*, lines 3164 and 3145.

THE ROW (page 131). "Each of us separate, both the same," varied in this poem, is from the wedding service in Judaism.

IN PLACE OF BELIEF (page 134). "You practice virtue without believing in it." Said, in the third person, of Dr. Larivière, who appears briefly, nobly, in Flaubert's *Madame Bovary*.

HARP SONG (page 142). Deor is a deposed court harpist in the Anglo-Saxon poem of that title. His poem's refrain is "thaes ofereode, thisses swa maeg," or "that is over; this will be, too."

Days of Wonder

REPENTANCE OF AN ART CRITIC, 1925 (page 147). *"Existe-t-il une peinture juive?* ("Is there a Jewish painting style?") In 1925, an article of that title by Fritz Vanderpyl appeared in *Mercure de France*, a Paris review. Vanderpyl asked "Where did it come from, and so suddenly, this desire to paint on the part of these descendants of the twelve tribes, this passion for paintbrush and palette, which—in spite of the Law—is being tolerated, even encouraged, in the most orthodox circles?" The poem was fueled by "Paris in New York: French Jewish Artists in Private Collections," an exhibit at the Jewish Museum.

JEWISH CEMETERY, ELEVENTH STREET (page 151). Second cemetery of the Spanish and Portuguese Synagogue, Shearith-Israel, 11th Street near Sixth Avenue. Founded in 1805, the burial ground was cut through in 1830, and only a wedge remains. Built in 1838, the Grapevine was a roadhouse frequented by artists.

The Paintings of Our Lives

MARGARET FULLER (page 169). Margaret Fuller drowned when her ship, the *Elizabeth,* struck the sands off Fire Island in 1850. With her were her husband, the marchese Giovanni Angelo Ossoli, and their child. Born in Boston in 1810, Fuller traveled to Italy in 1847, where she supported the revolution of the Roman Republic and wrote about it for the *New York Tribune.* I came upon the story of Fuller and the *Elizabeth* in Walt Whitman's notes about Long Island shipwrecks collected in *Specimen Days.* My information is gathered from the *Memoirs of Margaret Fuller Ossoli,* edited by Ralph Waldo Emerson (Phillips, Sampson, 1852), from Paula Blanchard's *Margaret Fuller* (Delacorte/Seymour Lawrence, 1978), and for my later revisions, Megan Marshall's important biography, *Margaret Fuller: A New American Life* (Houghton Mifflin, 2013).

BROOKLYN BRIDGE (page 172). Details about the bridge are from Alan Trachtenberg's *Brooklyn Bridge: Fact and Symbol* (Oxford University Press, 1965).

THE PAINTINGS OF OUR LIVES (page 179). *The Annunciation Altarpiece* (c.1425) by Robert Campin, the Flemish master, is also known as *The Annunciation Triptych, The Merode Altarpiece,* and *Robert Campin's Triptych.* It hangs in the

Cloisters, in New York, where it is called *The Annunciation Triptych*.

LAST REQUESTS (page 181). "Dorset, embrace him." Shakespeare's *Richard III*, act II, scene ii.

For That Day Only

FOOTSTEPS ON LOWER BROADWAY (page 192). Line 12: "I . . . headed for Pfaff's." Pfaff's Café. Charles Pfaff, owner; established 1856. In an interview, Whitman said: "I used to go to Pfaff's every night." *Brooklyn Daily Eagle*, 11 July 1866. Stanza 4, lines 40 through 50: In March 1842, Whitman attended services twice at the Shearith Israel Synagogue on Crosby Street, between Spring and Broome, in Lower Manhattan. Recounting both visits in the *Aurora* (March 28-29), Whitman wrote: "The heart within us felt awed as in the presence of memorials from an age that had passed away centuries ago. The strange and discordant tongue—the mystery, and all the associations that crowded themselves in troops upon our mind—made a thrilling sensation to creep through every nerve." Although Whitman does not refer to Judaism in his great poetic passages concerning world religions, he does incorporate Hebrew rhythms and imagery in his verse. Apparently the impact of Jewish ritual was deeper than he had supposed.

STONE DEMONS (page 203). Originally published as the third poem in "Bestiaries."

JULIAN OF NORWICH (page 207). Julian was a fourteenth-century anchorite who took her name from the parish church of St. Julian in Conisford at Norwich, an East Anglia town. "From a window in her cell she could view the Eucharist and from another window she could assist people seeking spiritual counsel" from *What Is Anglicanism?*, by Urban T. Holmes III (Morehouse-Barlow, 1982).

RESCUE IN PESCALLO (page 208). According to local tales, the statue of Christ in the Church of San Giacomo was washed up on the lakeshore. The details here are fictional.

Burn Down the Icons

SURELY AS CERTAINTY CHANGES (page 235). Stanza 3, line 2: "And proteolysis, 'the end of change/ Changing in the end.'" The term designates the enzymatic process by which protein is broken down.

LETTER TO HELEN (page 245). Helena Waldman-Gold, my father's sister, was a practicing pediatrician who declined to leave Warsaw even after the Nazi harassment of Jews in the 1930s. When World War II ended, my family learned, she had died in the Warsaw ghetto uprising in 1943. An Auschwitz survivor reported that Helen, believing she would be deported to a concentration camp, had climbed the tower of a municipal building, run to the ledge, pulled down the Polish flag from its staff, and ripped the flag to shreds. She stood for a while, holding the red cloth, before she was shot down by a Nazi guard. A survivor recounted her act to Helen's sister, my aunt Beta Snycer, who wrote from Israel, "It was an act of revenge on the Poles for having given her away." I've written about this story in an essay, "Helen" in *Testimony: Contemporary Writers Make the Holocaust Personal*, ed. by David Rosenberg (Random House, 1989). Section 2, line 10: "Awakening at last . . ." In Seneca's *Hercules Furens*, Hercules awakens to find he has committed murder in a fit of madness. Refusing to place blame on a god, he accepts responsibility. Section 3, line 1: "Will you say/Celan's 'Fadensonnen'?" This refers to *Poems* by Paul Celan, translated from the German by Michael Hamburger (Persea, 1988).

Acknowledgments

The author wishes to thank the following publications where some of these poems appeared.

Among the new poems:

Literary Matters: "Confessions," "Letter from Paul Celan," and "Scallop Shell."

The New Republic: "Night Visitor."

"Scallop Shell" is for Jody Asnes and Bruce Dow.

"Tesserae" is for Elizabeth Birkelund and Jonathan Marvel.

Among the Selected Poems:

Without a Claim (2013) first published by Houghton Mifflin Company. *The Broken String* (2007), *Days of Wonder* (2002), *The Paintings of Our Lives* (2001) first published by Houghton Mifflin Harcourt.

For That Day Only and *Hemispheres* first published by Sheep Meadow Press. *Burn Down the Icons* first published by Princeton University Press.

Grateful acknowledgment is made to the following journals where previously uncollected poems appeared:

American Scholar, The American Poetry Review, Antaeus, The Atlantic, Barrow Street, Boulevard, Cimarron Review, Cortland Review, DoubleTake, Fifth Wednesday, Forthcoming, Forward, The Georgia Review, Grand Street, The Guardian, The Hudson

Review, The Jewish Quarterly, The Kenyon Review, Literary Matters, Little Star, Michigan Quarterly, The Nation, New Letters, The New Republic, The New Yorker, The Ohio Review, The Paris Review, Pequod, Pleiades, Ploughshares, Plume Poetry, Poetry, Poetry Northwest, Prairie Schooner, Rattapallax, The Southampton Review, Shenandoah, The Texas Observer, Theology Today, Tikkun, TriQuarterly, Warwick Review, The Yale Review, Western Humanities Review.

I'm grateful to Baruch College, CUNY, for a fellowship leave that enabled me to finish this collection, and to the Bogliasco Foundation where new and recent poems were written. For their caring responses to poems in draft, I thank Alfred Corn, Megan Marshall, Emily McKeage, Carol Muske-Dukes, Elise Paschen, and Brian Swann. My thanks go to my friend and former editor, Pat Strachan, and to my research assistants, Jenna Breiter, Christine Degenaars, and Jiordan Castle. And above all, my gratitude goes to Ruth Greenstein, for her patience and wisdom.